Getting to
D.A.N.Y.

Getting to
D.A.N.Y.

Lessons from a New York Job Hunt

PAUL CAULFIELD

ISBN: 1540448029
ISBN 13: 9781540448026
Library of Congress Control Number: 2016920859
CreateSpace Independent Publishing Platform
North Charleston, South Carolina

Contents

Introduction · vii

Prologue ·xi

One   (Every) experience matters · 1

Two   Discover what you <u>don't</u> want· · · · · · · · · · · · · · · · · 7

Three   Try, even if it means failing · · · · · · · · · · · · · · · · 12

Four   Find a mentor· 31

Five   Do your homework · 41

Six   Get over yourself. Sometimes, you have to fake it· · · 51

Seven Choices are a luxury· 58

Eight At moments of truth, be yourself · · · · · · · · · · · · · · 63

Nine   When you're wrong, admit it · · · · · · · · · · · · · · · · 77

Ten   There's always a backstory · · · · · · · · · · · · · · · · · · 86

Epilogue· 107

Acknowledgements · 113

Appendix · 117

Bibliography & Suggested Reading · · · · · · · · · · · 125

About the Author· 127

Introduction

My first day as a Manhattan prosecutor fell on a Tuesday, September 4, 2001.

For a transplant from suburban Maryland, New York City was a shift into overdrive. Learning to prosecute crimes, more so. But after what happened a week later and for the rest of my time working for the New York County District Attorney's Office… to describe that? I'll quote (now old) Brooklyn, *fuhgeddaboudit.*

As the years pass, I've marveled at how the task of just getting there, the job <u>hunt</u>, was so flat out humbling. I've recognized a universality, as well. So many first-time job seekers – and job seekers in general – have war stories. Whether they're funny, debasing, joyous or sad, they're all offered as unique.

Why is that?

I think it's because these stories are our silver lining to a certain flawed thinking – that what we do professionally somehow encapsulates who we are as people. *So...what do you do?* is our less scientific Myers-Briggs personality test. Maybe that's one reason why job searches are so difficult, we want *just the right one.*

Whatever that means.

Roughly a year and a half after I left the D.A.'s Office, I was reading *The New York Post* walking home from the train. It was Friday, February 3, 2006. I stopped and stared at the headline on page 21.

"He Died Doing What He Loved."

Under it was a black and white photograph of New York City Police Officer Kevin Lee. A "true blue cop," it said. Lee had collapsed and died the week prior chasing a suspect. He was only thirty-one years old. I tore out the page and over that weekend began looking through a journal I kept while in law school and during my time as a prosecutor.

Officer Lee was one of the first cops I had met on the job, and he delighted in calling me "rookie," even after my first year. I smile thinking of his mischievous grin, popping into my office just so he could call it out before moving on to his other prosecutors and cases.

As I looked at earlier entries, the ones from law school, I was struck by the stress and doubt I felt as graduation approached and I looked for work. The irony, with the benefit of time, is that so much of it was self-inflicted.

I had respectable grades. I had a few but important life and work experiences. More importantly, I had supportive parents and a great family. I was also newly married to a woman I loved, and most importantly, she was employed!

I'll say this, too…now. It was a foregone conclusion I would get a job. I just had to stay after it. Each version of my résumé, each lead, each interview, every "thank you" was a step forward. Not knowing from whom or when (or if) an offer would come, though, plunged the journey into darkness.

So, this short book, *Getting to D.A.N.Y.*

In examining the challenge of the job search, particularly as a first-timer and one pursuing the opportunity of a lifetime investigating and prosecuting crimes in New York City, I realized the power of a basic sentiment. I'll paraphrase a prayer I learned in high school:

Parts of life are out of our control. Period. Other parts, we can manage and even mold. If we can find the time to think, reflect or even pray, we might be able to discern the difference. Hopefully, we can then find the strength to acknowledge the inability on the one hand, while rolling up our sleeves and getting to work on the other.

As the title indicates, this book is not about the Manhattan D.A.'s Office, itself. There are some insights into its recent and (very) distant pasts, and I hope you enjoy reading them as much as I enjoyed putting them together.

For privacy's sake throughout, I've used only a few actual names, including former District Attorney Robert M. Morgenthau. Dates are approximations, and where the few criminal cases are concerned, I combined details from various cases. To identify defendants or victims would be self-serving, legally improper or both.

I was a New York prosecutor for three years, leaving in the fall of 2004. I learned a lot there, and it was the greatest (and toughest) job I've had. My fellow rookies and I knew we were experiencing something special given the place, the time and the man at the helm. Some day, someone will write that story.

For now, here is one of just getting to D.A.N.Y.

Paul Caulfield
New York City
October 25, 2016

Prologue

The Manhattan D.A.'s Office

It's December 2000, and Martin Luther King, Jr. is standing there, staring. His gaze falls with the intensity of the sun and a magnifying glass. There he is, across the room.

He's in a photo, of course, but his stare, I swear, is the Mona Lisa incarnate. It tightens my newly acquired tie.

His face is so round.

I'm in a crisp new suit.

I crane forward and crush the suit, trying to get a better look. He's shorter and softer than I recall from history books. I never really stared at his picture. But there he is. Dressed in a dark suit shaking hands with a young white man with thick black rimmed glasses – a sign of the 1960s' conservative side.

King's famous at this point. He's already boycotted racially divided buses in Alabama. It's unclear whether he's marched on Washington, yet, where everyone heard his Dream, or been awarded the Nobel Peace Prize, one of the youngest recipients ever. It doesn't matter. I know he has.

The man who's next to him is not so famous. Not yet. Ten years older than King, Robert M. Morgenthau is a federal prosecutor for New York. Officially, U.S. Attorney for New York's Southern District. President Kennedy appointed him shortly after taking office. President Johnson will later make the easy decision to reappoint him.

Morgenthau is wired politically. Henry, his father, was long-time Secretary of the Treasury to Franklin Roosevelt. Morgenthau's grandfather, Henry, Sr., served another Democrat, Woodrow Wilson, during World War I as Ambassador to the Ottoman Empire after making a fortune in real estate.

Though often the case when scions of accomplished men approach the mantle of power, privilege or both, Robert Morgenthau is no lightweight. Following college, Amherst, he enlisted in the Navy and the Second World War raging at the time. Within five years he ascended to the rank of Lieutenant Commander.

More notably, he descended into the April waters of the Mediterranean Sea when his destroyer, the U.S.S. Lansdale, was split in two by German torpedoes in the spring of 1944.

It was there on the early morning of 21 April while treading water for four hours that Morgenthau made a well-reported pact with God. Should he survive, he would dedicate his life's work to public service.

Following the Navy, Morgenthau entered law school, Yale, and then private practice in New York City where he stayed until making partner in 1954. He remained partner for another seven years before being tapped by Kennedy, two years his senior, to be the region's chief federal prosecutor in 1961.

Morgenthau's life of public service was born.

I lean back.

I won't meet King. But the simply framed, black and white photograph of King and the young prosecutor vibrates.

It's December 14, 2000. King is gone.

I will meet Morgenthau, though. At any moment.

I want to join his office.

I'm twenty-six years old and in my last year of law school. Morgenthau's no longer a federal prosecutor. That, too, has passed. He is District Attorney for Manhattan. Officially, New York County. It's an office he took when I was *one* and has made into the country's premier prosecutor's office.

Paul Caulfield

As I sit in the waiting room just outside his office in Lower Manhattan, the eyes of other dignitaries since passed, dozens of them, peer my way from every angle on every wall of the small room.

Some are known to me. To everyone. John F. Kennedy. *Bobby*, reportedly a good friend. Mayors Koch and Dinkins, I should know but do not. I'm not a New Yorker. But no matter the face – instantly recognizable, vaguely familiar or totally foreign – there's Morgenthau again and again and again.

The beaten to submission, cracked leather couch I'm on is in cahoots with the pictures. It won't let me relax. With its worn, tissued skin, it sucks me in. This is a piece of furniture that surely entered the office when its boss did in 1975.

To complicate matters, my rear end is a foot below the couch's sea level. My knees shoot skyward forming a checkmark of an ass-to-knees contortion that reconfigures my suit to the point of absurdity. Made of off the rack wool, my jacket and pants have hiked themselves up to create an interesting billow of untailored material around my shoulders and exploding inconveniently above my lap.

I play in my head how the meeting will go down. I cling to the repeated assurances that having been granted this, the fourth and final interview, an offer of Assistant District Attorney is all but certain.

As simple as that.

"I'm making you an offer," he will reportedly say with a take-it-or-leave-it finality that warns the receiver to not tempt fate and accept on the spot.

Lore has it that only once did a candidate seated beside the "Boss," as he's been referred to these past eighteen months, fail to hear those words. As I heard it, the near prosecutor broke the cardinal rule of trial law and asked a question she didn't know the answer to.

Rather than an offer, she received silence and the exit door.

Her mistake?

She presumed the photograph of the young girl on the aged D.A.'s desk was his granddaughter and not his child.

It's taken me years to get here.

I'd love to say it began with my own pact with God while treading water in the dark Mediterranean on an early morning.

It didn't.

It began with a challenge from a former nun when I was twenty-three. We weren't in the water. We were sitting in tiny kid seats at a tiny kid table in a Durán, Ecuador daycare.

Suddenly, Robert Morgenthau appeared in the doorway.

Ungracefully, I detached myself from the couch.

The interview was on.

One

(Every) experience matters

Durán, Durán

Fairfield University is New England and Jesuit. In the spring of 1996, I was a senior. Like most seniors, I had little idea what I'd be doing come that June. So, come that June, like a Jesuit, I moved to South America. That decision, and one particular experience, later became the single best case I would make to become a Manhattan prosecutor.

Durán, Ecuador wasn't a city or town. It was a collection of *barrios*, neighborhoods, strewn over a hillside and then flatland opposite Guayaquil, the country's second largest city. The Guayas River separated them and a hundred years.

The word *sprawling* is appropriate for Durán of the mid '90s. With a documented population of one-hundred and fifty thousand people and another fifty thousand or so undocumented for good measure, Durán was wooden shacks on stilts and the well-to-do in cinder blocks. It was open pits as sewers along dirt roads, electrical wires strung by a drunk and stores plastered with that week's presidential candidates vowing radical reforms for *los pobres*, the poor. It was wandering cows and homeless chickens, chilled water running from cisterns atop corrugated tin roofs to kitchen sinks and shower heads.

In August 1996, this was my home. For one year, I was *un misionero Catolico* as it said on my Ecuadorian driver's license. There was no bible thumping, though. The country was ninety-five percent Catholic; we won. Two Mormons who lived around the corner made a nice go of it though, visiting us and our Ecuadorian neighbors with a frequency and zeal that would have made St. Ignatius of Loyola blush.

I was there, literally, to hang out with locals. Unlike its non-secular counterpart, the Peace Corps, our program required a commitment to pray daily, lead a simple life and create your own contributions.

"Be the face of Christ," our program's director instructed us before we left the states. "In everything you do. With everyone you meet. Let them see Christ."

No pressure.

Getting to D.A.N.Y.

The first three months were a misery. Hanging out, it turned out, was hard. First, there was the language.

It wasn't English.

I arrived confident that I spoke Spanish. I quickly discovered...I couldn't *speak* Spanish. I could *say words* in Spanish. I could even choke out a few sentences. But attempting to drive my jalopy of a second language on the autobahn left me sputtering. New friends blew past me with souped up native fluency.

In body only, I was part of conversations with friends and locals. In every facet, though, I was disconnected as my brain scrambled to keep up. For the first brutal weeks, I got just a morsel of what was whizzing by as I stood there all but deaf and dumb. It ruined my days.

Within a few weeks, I was teaching English in a Durán parish, re-stocking medicine and playing dominoes at a Hansen's Disease (leprosy) hospital in Guayaquil and working in a children's soup kitchen north of the city. I was fried at each day's end.

Exhaustion came from speaking and silently, frantically, constantly translating what was said in return. Emotionally, I was drained by the depths of malnourished babies, pregnant children and abusive, drunk husbands. I was staggered by the heights of the gratitude from a young leper for just talking with her, the serenity from prayer and the satisfaction of finally holding a telephone conversation in another language. Life became complex. It improved also.

Blink.

The year ended. As it did, I surprisingly found myself considering the priesthood. A former nun unknowingly helped me decide against it.

Samantha McNulty, an ex-pat from Louisiana, ran an elite private school in a suburban enclave of Guayaquil. In its twentieth year, the school was known for its demanding and bi-lingual curriculum, state of the art technology and varsity athletics. Admission guaranteed access to top U.S. schools. The sons and daughters of Guayaquil's elite clamored to get in and wore attending as a mark of success. Sam admitted them, charging the parents in kind.

She admitted others, too. Less wealthy. The poor sons and daughters of Durán. Sam charged these families nothing, bused them in by the hundreds and gave them uniforms, books and pencils, free lunches and healthcare. She employed dads as bus drivers and janitors. Moms taught *keen-dair* and *pre-keen-dair* for the youngest students. Those unemployable, Sam offered classes.

The poor who graduated got jobs. One went to the United States to study. Then another. Then another. Odds being what they were, not everyone succeeded. A student of mine, a seventh grader, stopped coming to school in the spring of 1997. At twelve years old, she had been eager to fit in. Shy. A wonderful smile.

While walking along a dirt road, I happened to pass her house, a cement square with curtains. A typical scene for unemployed women in the barrio, she (oddly not her mother) was standing in the windowless opening watching life. After a few steps, I saw why. She was pregnant.

The girl I had known was fading and her demeanor odd as we spoke. She was a toddler too confident in the high heels of her mother. She was *I'm sorry*. She was *This is what is expected of me*. Then, she was gone.

At dinner the night before I left for home, I brought this up. To Sam, it was familiar. That's why she was there…in her twentieth year. To Sam, I was familiar. She had seen me, my type, swoop in year after year and, twelve months later, swoop out largely over-inflated. My "journey" was Sam's reality. I could leave and would in nine hours. Sam would finish out her life in Ecuador, founder of a new world for Durán's families. As she must have done every year, she drew back this curtain.

"The life you left in the states is going to look a lot different," she said. "That's a good thing. But promise me that when you get home, you'll get a good job and make lots of money. When you do, promise me that you'll remember the people you've met and help those who can't do it themselves."

I promised.

I got a good job.

I forgot to make lots of money.

In August 1997, I returned to my parents' home in Kensington, Maryland and took a job teaching religion in a Washington, D.C. parish. That year, I applied and was accepted to law school for the fall of 1998.

Two

Bitter with the Sweet!

It took me the first half of law school to figure out I wanted to be a prosecutor. One professor knew at the start what I wasn't going to be.

"How many of you know what you want to do when you graduate?" Kevin Crosby asked us our first day of Legal Writing.

Crosby had no interest in teaching us how to write "like lawyers" yet.

A few hands from around the lecture hall shot into the air. Others wavered.

"Mr....Caulfield," he said, looking up from the soon-to-be ubiquitous seating chart resting on the podium.

"What are you going to do?"

I tried to sound confident, relaxed. "I'd like to be a family lawyer."

"Why?"

"Well, I like the idea of having a small practice near where I grew up. Help my friends buy their houses...write their wills...."

I wanted to be their go-to guy. Defend their kids when they screwed up, their trusted friend with the law degree.

"You're not going to be a family lawyer," he said. He returned to the seating chart and repeated his exercise. After a few rounds, we got the message.

"Chances are you will do something in law you never intended," Crosby said. "Chart a few paths these next three years. You'll be surprised what you find."

The following fall, I was standing in the basement of a small law office in Rockville, Maryland when I discovered I didn't want to be a family lawyer.

Getting to D.A.N.Y.

Consisting of three partners, Michaels, Quick & Thomson was a mix of civil, criminal and family law, cigarette smoke and coarse humor, curt directives and insta-errands to the bank, the court and the accident scene. It offered the perfect antidote to the mirage that I and other second year students had begun to project with great gusto – that we actually knew something about the law.

Thomson summed up nicely my array of duties, which in addition to budding law clerk included errand boy, calling out from his office, "Bitter with the sweet!" whenever I passed by attending to the less glamorous.

I was getting coffee for a client.

"Bitter with the sweet!"

Taking client checks to the bank.

"Bitter with the sweet!"

Making copies.

"Bitter with the sweet!"

I was in the basement making copies.

A cardboard box with hundreds of documents, discovery from an ongoing divorce, sat on a nearby table, bursting. With various sized paper assembled in piles, the automatic feeder was out. I was making copies...

one...

painful...

page...

at a time.

Resigned to my fate, a game mercifully unfolded.

The object: to press "Copy" at perfect intervals so the scanner passed under the glass without pausing, eliciting a *whirr-thirrt, whirr-thirrt* cadence.

The challenge: to stay in stride with the page-being-copied... button-being-pushed...page-being-replaced speed of a symphony conductor on coke.

I swayed from cardboard box to machine and back again, my heart racing, a likely first for Xerox. Hot paper poured steadily onto the tray below. It was mesmerizing.

The golden tempo, I admired.

The awkwardness of artwork and stiff paper halted everything. Red construction paper folded into a long greeting card.

A half sheet of lined writing paper was pasted inside. Its whole design stirred giddy images of *Happy Valentine's Day! Hugs and kisses!! I love you!!!!!!!!!!!!!!!!!!*

It wasn't.

It was about *Daddy.*

And *Mommy.*

And *So angry.*

Why yelling?

Stop fighting!

Screaming in the scrawling hand of a child, *It makes me sooooooo sad!!!!*

Work wasn't so fun anymore.

One card didn't do it. I had seen others, and that was part of it. Knock down, drag 'em out divorces were also. Not what I cared for. Civil suits and personal injury. Not what I cared for. Defending.

Not what I cared for.

Three

TRY, EVEN IF IT MEANS FAILING

My Man Here

P rosecuting.

It wasn't immediate. It appeared my first semester in Criminal Law. It caught my attention in Criminal Procedure the next. By the summer of 1999 in Evidence, I was hooked. Despite this, the very idea of getting into a courtroom brought a mixture of terror and exhilaration that reminded me of a Jerry Seinfeld bit.

Claiming that the number one fear of Americans was speaking in public, Seinfeld, in one of the familiar teasers that began his sitcom, asked the audience what they thought the second fear was.

Someone in the crowd guessed it.

Dying.

As Seinfeld saw it, everyone at a funeral would rather be in the coffin than giving the eulogy.

The Catholic University of America's law school recognized something similar and wanted its students practicing law immediately. By second year, no one could schedule classes on Tuesdays or Thursdays. The implication – get to work. For those interested in criminal defense or prosecution, it meant get in court.

The time it took me to try my first case was bested only by the speed it took to go south. It was January 2000, and I was working as a student prosecutor in the Maryland State's Attorney's Office.

Under a state administrative rule, "Rule Sixteen", law students had the ability to appear in court and were granted the authority of prosecutors. Similar to the authority granted to sixteen year old drivers, they also had real prosecutors sitting shotgun, second chair, in the event they *wheeee!* steered wildly off course.

Shawn Carrings, my supervising prosecutor, was a fourth year Assistant State's Attorney. A few months shy of moving up from less serious cases, the routine-ness of it all was apparent.

In a barren office in Upper Marlboro, Maryland sat cases, piles of fifty, each representing a day's status hearings and dispositions. Dubbed the "rocket docket" for the speed in which the judge dispatched a day's cases, a particular day typically ended by lunch.

Understandably so. Any given week was a merry-go-round of three offenses – hurting someone, damaging something or taking something.

You hit someone.

Assault.

But she wasn't hurt.

Attempted assault.

Actually, you missed.

Harassment.

But you broke her glasses.

Criminal mischief.

You also took her cell phone.

Petit larceny.

You called her house, but she hung up. So…you called again and again and again.

Menacing.

You followed her to work.

Stalking.

Keyed her car.

Criminal mischief.

Later, you took something from a store and hid it in your pocket…

Petit larceny.

…but dropped it when the guard saw you…

Attempted petit larceny.

…but broke it when you kicked it under a shelf.

Criminal mischief.

And broke the guard's finger when he grabbed you.

Assault.

But didn't mean it!

Reckless assault.

I picked up a file. It was an assault case. One person caused physical injury to another. In this case, he did it intentionally. In this case, the owner of a car dealership (the defendant) pushed and then hit one of his mechanics (the victim). It hurt the victim. So said the allegations.

"Always add lesser charges," Shawn said as we sorted the cases. "You want to prove the top count. If you can't, you've got something else to hang on to."

It was now an assault case, an attempted assault case and a one-size-fits-all disorderly conduct case.

The courtroom was packed the next day. At twenty-five years old, being part of court let alone walking into one was completely foreign. A line of defendants had habitually formed, beginning at the prosecutor's table in the well, fifteen feet from the judge's bench, and ending somewhere beyond the room's double doors.

Questions about case times peppered us as we wormed our way through the reluctantly parting crowd. Shawn moved forward unfazed and deaf to the repeated inquiries directed at *him*, because they *knew* who I was, falling in behind, awkwardness in tow.

Once at the table, I unpacked the case files, projecting too much seriousness while I arranged and then re-arranged them. Shawn stood off to the side idly chatting with a court officer about the latest woes of the Washington Wizards. He looked over and motioned to get going.

With one of his first pieces of advice still fresh in my mind, I turned to the crowd.

"Good morning, ladies and gentlemen!"

Backs straightened.

"My name is Paul Caulfield, and I am with the State's Attorney's Office. When you hear your name, please say, 'Here'. Save all questions until your case is called."

It was odd to shout in the faces of so many people I could have whispered to. But there was no doubt the same crowd forty feet away heard me perfectly.

I bowed my head and read through roll call. As I did, a new, albeit ridiculous, satisfaction came over me. I had said a few basic sentences in an open courtroom.

Within minutes of the judge taking the bench, we were rolling.

"People, is there an offer?"

I looked at the file and made an offer. There was always an offer.

"Yes, Judge, a hundred and twenty-five dollars in restitution and the stet docket."

"Yes, Judge, three days community service and the stet docket."

"Yes, Judge, five alcohol awareness classes and the stet docket."

The stet docket was very popular. Do something to make amends, the State will put aside the case for six months. Don't screw up, the case goes away. As often as an offer included pleading guilty to a charge – typically disorderly conduct, harassment or attempted petit larceny – the stet docket was the fan favorite.

Court hummed along.

The court officer called the case.

The defendant and attorney (if there was one) walked to the defense table.

Is there an offer?

Offer.

[Cue the defense attorney.]

"Your Honor, at this time my client would like to withdraw his previously entered plea of 'not guilty' and enter a plea of 'guilty' to…"

[Repeat]

This isn't so hard!

[Repeat]

Feeling lawyerly!

[Repeat]

Look at me! I'm prosecuting!

Then…

"Your Honor, the People offer ten days community service, five anger management classes and a disorderly conduct." Total autopilot.

The defendant laughed and shook his head.

I looked over.

It was the car dealer who hit his mechanic.

The defense attorney lowered his file and exhaled.

"Judge, though that's a *very* gracious offer, it's *totally* inappropriate in this case."

The judge looked at me and then Shawn.

"Please approach."

Out of earshot of the defendant and court reporter, the judge flipped through her own case file. Shawn, the defense attorney and I leaned in.

The judge gave a half-shake of her head.

"This man has no criminal record," she said. "He's forty-seven...married...with three children. He's owned the dealership for...what....eighteen years."

She closed the file and looked at me.

"I am not making him do ten days of community service. Two, three nights of anger management, fine. I also don't think a disorderly conduct is appropriate here."

She turned to Shawn.

"Do you, Mr. Carrings?"

"Yes, Judge, I do," Shawn replied matter-of-factly.

Undeterred, she continued.

"Here's what I propose. Let's put this on the stet docket. Mr. Mitchell attends three anger management classes and pays a one hundred dollar fine. If he attends the classes and pays the fine, we'll dismiss the case in six months."

She looked at each of us, satisfied, the matter settled. The defense attorney agreed.

"That sounds very reasonable, Judge. I'm sure Henry will accept that. He'd like to put this unfortunate incident behind him."

The judge turned to Shawn.

"People?"

"I'm sorry, Judge. The best we can do is a discon. The three days and hundred dollar fine are OK, just not the stet."

The defense attorney spoke, "Judge…"

The judge cut him off, lifting her hand.

"Fine," she said.

The word dropped from her lips like lead. The little warmth she had shown, gone.

"My offer is now withdrawn. This case will go to trial…today. And, I am telling you right now…I will not find Mr. Mitchell guilty. Is that clear?"

Her forehead and shoulders aimed all firepower at Shawn.

"That's fine, Judge. My man here will try the case," he said as his hand landed on my shoulder.

She swiveled and recalibrated.

"Fine," she said, burning a hole in my face.

"We'll finish the docket, and then this case will go to trial. Step. Back."

Shawn spoke as we turned away.

"We've just been hijacked. She does it all the time."

Finishing the docket was a game of chess an hour before execution. I grappled to make things better. The judge's asides to the court officers became witty and head-shakingly, *You're-too-much-Judge! Ha!...ha-ha-ha!!!* funny.

Her counter-offers became learned and gracious compared to my shallowly-proposed offers that wallowed in the muck of ignorance. They disgusted me.

You are wise, I emoted, squinting from the glare of her being.

All senses were in overdrive to somehow, and at present telepathically, change the course I had been strapped into by my co-pilot now deeply engaged in a tri-folded sports page masquerading as a case file.

As soon as we finished the docket, the court officer tightened the noose.

"Recalling case number thirty-nine, 'People of the State of Maryland versus Henry Mitchell'."

The defense attorney and soon-to-be-acquitted Henry Mitchell rose from the gallery and strode to their table. Shawn passed them on his way out.

"I'll be back here," he said, closing the low wooden gate, now separating himself from the proceeding.

"What?" I said, turning.

"You'll be fine," he called over his shoulder. He then slipped into a back row.

"People, you may proceed," the judge said.

I turned back to face the judge. Too panicked to be nervous, I jumped in.

"Uh, the facts are simple, your Honor..."

I should have added two sentences and sat down. An abusive car dealer gave his smaller mechanic a black eye and stitches. And he did so intentionally.

I didn't.

I went on and delivered an epic volume of legal proselytizing and courtroom pop culture.

"It is the People's contention, your Honor...

...the facts will prove, your Honor...

…this Court will find, your Honor…"

I casually strode toward the judge's bench. *See! I'm not scared!* A stream of consciousness poured from me. Two minutes in the judge had heard enough.

"People, call your first witness."

"Yes, Judge."

Michael Rios was my first and only witness.

The victim.

He was a slight Hispanic from Honduras. He was also no help.

His injuries since healed, Rios thought his *machismo* was on trial and not the guy who had punched him in the face.

I dragged the basics out of him, his displeasure of testifying against his manhood on full display. In clipped sentences, he described how he had worked at the dealership for a year and a half and how he and the dealer began shouting at each other about a broken car door on a new BMW.

"What happened next?" I asked.

"When I wasn't lookin', he hit me," he said.

"Where did he hit you?"

"Here."

"Could you please…" I said.

"Let the record reflect that Mr. Rios has indicated an area around his left eye," the judge intoned robotically.

The court reporter clacked away.

"Thank you, Judge," I said.

"Continue."

"Could you please describe the pain you felt…" I began.

"Objection," the defense attorney said.

"Sustained," chimed the judge.

I looked at the judge. I had no idea what I'd done wrong. I tried again.

"Mr. Rios, could you please tell the judge about the pain…"

"Objection," the defense attorney said.

"Sustained," she chimed again.

The oven in my suit clicked on.

I tried again to get the victim to describe the pain of being hit in the face.

"Objection."

"Sustained."

Every eye in the room looked on, amused as I crashed against an invisible fence.

"Objection."

"Sustained."

Beaten and now in full fever, I looked at the judge.

What am I doing wrong?

"People, you're *leading* the witness…what pain? You haven't established a proper foundation."

The witness looked on.

I turned and asked the largely pointless but required question.

"Mr. Rios, please describe how you felt when you were hit."

"It didn't hurt," he offered eagerly.

The defense attorney sat up and beamed at his continued good fortune.

"It didn't hurt?" I said.

How is this getting worse?

"Naw."

I turned and looked at Shawn, now also sitting up.

Is this a joke?

I turned back to the "victim".

"You were punched in the face, and it didn't hurt?"

Rios looked down and shook his head in pity for the defendant's long ago effort.

"Naw. It was just lucky."

"Were you injured?"

"A little."

"What were your injuries?" I said feeling a glimmer of hope.

"I had a cut."

"Where?"

"Here."

"Did you have to see…"

"Let the record reflect Mr. Rios is again indicating an area around his left eye."

"I'm sorry, Judge," I said.

"That's ok. Go on," she said, her own pity now on display.

Rios lamely admitted needing stitches but offered one final, "It didn't hurt," just in case anyone had missed it.

"Thank you, Mr. Rios," I lied.

"I have no more questions."

"Your witness," the judge said.

"No questions, your honor," the defense attorney said. *The prosecution has done enough.*

"Fine, I will now hear closing arguments," the judge responded.

The defense attorney was brief.

"…an unfortunate incident, yes, your Honor. Not one where Henry Mitchell intentionally assaulted anyone. We ask that you find Mr. Mitchell 'not guilty' on all counts."

The defense attorney was actually glowing as he sat down.

I, too, was brief, sticking mainly to the facts. The moment I finished, the judge gave her verdict.

"I find the defendant 'not guilty.' Mr. Mitchell, have a pleasant afternoon. The Court will now be in recess until nine-thirty tomorrow morning."

The judge then stood, lightly tapped the desk with her pen and vanished into her chambers.

Four

I was a Kung Fu Archer

I tried roughly a dozen cases as a Rule Sixteen prosecutor. The cases didn't get easier. Defense attorneys, typically experienced, made sure of it. It went beyond a better understanding of the law and courtroom procedure.

From some – the jaded – there were subtle, and not so subtle, put downs zeroing in on my youth and inexperience. Others were outright bullies. This was life, *how things got done,* and they knew it. Some openly relished it.

"Just keep trying cases," Shawn said. "Hold your ground."

So, each time he saw an opportunity, I tried a case. Generally, he sat in the back, and whether I stunk or made a decent argument, he supported my efforts. On one occasion, a judge called me to the bench following closing arguments.

With a wink and a whisper, he said, "You've got it," and it thrilled me to no end.

Improving meant, more than anything else, getting comfortable in court. Sustained objections meant, *OK, let's try it this way,* with less wattage radiating from self-consciousness.

Verbal barbs penetrated less. Mostly, though, the lessons learned in Evidence, Criminal Procedure and Trial Advocacy came alive and revealed a glimpse of what mastering them could unlock. I was hooked.

I was a year from graduation when I finished that second spring semester. Like everyone else, I began to hunt madly for a job. I naively thought the search would merely be an exercise in which prosecutor's office would accept me. I knew which one I wanted, though.

The Manhattan District Attorney's Office.

Officially known as the District Attorney's Office for New York County, D.A.N.Y. employed over five hundred lawyers. Each year it brought in a rookie class of some sixty new attorneys usually fresh from law school or a judicial clerkship. A few came from private firms wanting a change from the grind of associate life.

Getting to D.A.N.Y.

The hiring process was famously grueling. Broken into four stages, an initial pool of some fifteen hundred candidates submitted applications at the start of their third year. Quite automatically, a large portion was granted an initial interview typically held one-on-one with traveling prosecutors on law school campuses throughout the country.

From there, major culling began as selected candidates received invitations to sit before a panel of prosecutors a few weeks later in Manhattan. While there, they were subjected to an onslaught of courtroom hypotheticals and legal one-ups-manship that poked and prodded one's understanding of New York law, ability to perform mental gymnastics and, especially, grace under fire.

The few who survived were then asked to sit before Michelle Dylan, a completely no-nonsense prosecutor, for the third and most piercing interview. Many candidates left her office broken having come so close. The successful ones left on the cusp of appointment with the fourth and final interview with the "Boss," District Attorney Robert M. Morgenthau, a reported formality.

The job, only then, was theirs to lose. So lore went.

The application was straightforward.

I already had a résumé, which I had labored over intensely in response to the universal refrain that, "It's your first writing sample."

At the start of my final year, I asked my wife, Alyssa, to look it over one night. We were newly married. I readied my glove for a softball.

She lined a screamer.

"Three pages?" she said, curling up on the couch.

"What? No good?"

She flipped through the pages. "It's a bit too long, don't you think?"

She looked up, "You taught *karate?*"

"I did."

"You *know* karate?"

The inflections were killing me.

"I helped the instructor..." I said.

"That was twelve years ago. You were..."

"Fourteen."

"I'm not sure that's worth keeping."

She read on. After a few tortured minutes, she semi-offered the pages.

"Do you mind if I work on this?" she said. "Try and get it to a page?"

The urge to snatch the loose papers and scurry upstairs was overwhelming.

"It's not good?" I asked.

"It's fine."

I didn't hear her say "fine".

"Save it as a new version," I mustered.

A few days later she handed me a completely new document.

One page.

Tight.

"This looks great," I said as my eyes scrolled the page.

Something was missing.

"Being a certified archery instructor isn't important?"

"It is," she said, reaching out and touching the paper's edge, "but this…this is the most important."

A few days later, I was granted my first interview with the Manhattan D.A.'s Office. September 28, 2000. It was in a wing on campus that I had never laid foot in. The door to the meeting room opened, and Dave Christopher, another third year, stepped out.

"How did it go?"

"Great. He's really nice. Funny. Good luck."

"Thanks," I said, moving through the door.

The room was small with tan walls and one window looking onto the law school's driveway. A smiling, middle aged man sat at a round table. He extended his hand and through a graying beard said, "Ernie Mitchell."

"Paul Caulfield."

"Nice to meet you. Have a seat."

His voice and manner were warm. I was grateful. It then began like any job interview.

"So Paul, tell me, why do you want to be a New York County Assistant District Attorney?"

If I knew one thing, I knew that. I had thought about it for months, spoken with current and former Manhattan prosecutors as well as prosecutors from any other office who would speak with me. Whether they were still working as Assistant D.A.s or left years ago, it was all the same.

Prosecutors loved being prosecutors. Prosecutors also loved speaking about being prosecutors. But, out of all the prosecutors I spoke to, Kyle Miller trumped them all.

An attorney I had worked for put me in touch with Kyle in the spring of 2000. Eight years a Manhattan prosecutor, he was my first contact with the office. He also proved to be the most helpful.

"It's the best job in the world," he said, his voice crackling through the phone the first time I spoke with him.

"I've been out four years now, and I still miss it. My wife used to get so pissed when we watched *Law & Order*. She won't let me watch it any more...or any other crime show."

"So, why do you want to be a prosecutor?" Kyle continued.

I dipped a toe in the water.

"Well, I'm currently a student prosecutor in Maryland ..."

"Good," came his response.

"…I love the courtroom…"

"Great. Great. What else?"

"…in prosecution I've seen a lot of dedicated people…"

"Nice. Now why do you want to be a *New York County* prosecutor?"

"Because it's the premier prosecutor's office in the country," I said, reciting a line from its website.

"So? Why else?" he asked, unmoved.

"Because I like that there's a tradition of working above agendas and politics…" I said, referring to the office's mid-century battles with Tammany Hall and, later, the mafia.

"Nice. You've been doing your homework," he said.

"Yeah."

"Good. Great. What else?"

"Because it's a great first step out of law school…"

"No!" he shouted.

"What? What's wrong with that?"

"Listen," Kyle said. I imagined him sitting on the edge of his seat gripping the phone.

"This job has a three year commitment. For a reason. If you break it, kiss your legal career goodbye. You could go somewhere else, sure. Earn more money. That's not why you do it. You do it because every day you will literally sprint to work. You'll hate to leave at night. I mean it when I say it, it's the greatest job in the world. But the pay is killer. That's why there's a commitment. The last thing you want to say is that the D.A.'s Office is a stepping stone. Whether you're going to stay three years or thirty, when you go into that interview, you're a lifer."

I wasn't so sure about thirty, but three years was a piece of cake. So I thought.

Now Ernie Mitchell was asking me the same question, and it was new again.

Please don't screw this up.

I rushed my answer. I talked about traveling to Ecuador and then teaching and a growing desire to help others. As I did, something clicked, and the butterflies flew away.

"But why New York?" Ernie asked.

"Where would you rather be?" I half laughed, which made me worry I was being too comfortable.

I spoke about the thrill of New York City.

"That by itself could be my answer," I said.

I also told him about Alyssa, a New Yorker and only child. I was one of four sons. As much as I wanted this for me professionally, I wanted it for her personally.

"…of all the prosecutors' offices in the world…" I said, offering an empty hand before trailing off.

We spoke for another five minutes.

"Very nice to meet you, Paul," Ernie said, extending his hand, again.

"We'll be in touch."

I opened the door, and the next person filed in. After the door closed, it dawned on me in the empty hallway.

Ernie Mitchell hadn't asked a single legal question.

Five

Do your homework

Mental Gymnastics

I sought out Dave Christopher. He had the same experience.

I called Kyle.

"Ernie's a great guy. Trial Bureau 40, I think. You're fine. He just wanted to see if he liked you."

He finished with, "Keep me posted."

I didn't feel fine.

The days and weeks following the interview took on a Jekyll and Hyde quality as the predictable pattern of classes revving up

Paul Caulfield

to final exams became distorted by nights and weekends and then mornings and class times searching for work.

The passive act of submitting applications, résumés and cover letters became an all-consuming hunt made all the more dizzying with near-weekly train rides from Maryland to New York for interviews with prosecutors' offices in the city and on Long Island.

At every moment, I rode any current to broadcast my strengths – trial work in Maryland's criminal courts and, now in my third year, clerking for a federal prosecutor in Washington, D.C. – and mute a weakness I would have traded anything not to have – average grades.

With the focus on New York, an additional task presented itself, showing that I knew that state's criminal laws and not just the generic ones pounded into me and every other law student across the nation.

Every law student knew *Brady v. Maryland*, the 1963 U.S. Supreme Court case directing prosecutors to *cut it out* and just tell their defendants about any evidence they had that proved the defendants' claims (and undercut theirs).

New York followed that ruling.

Everyone had heard, "You have the right to remain silent…"

Law students knew it as another Supreme Court case, this time out of Arizona involving a guy named Miranda in 1966.

New York followed that one, too.

It followed more local rulings, as well. Ones I studied during my laps on Amtrak.

Question: Can prosecutors tell juries about a defendant's past crimes?

Answer: Maybe... Would those past crimes show why he committed the current crime or that the crime wasn't an accident?

If so, then yes. Otherwise it was just piling on. *People v. Molineux.* (New York, 1901.)

Question: Do prosecutors have to disclose their witnesses' statements before trial?

Answer: Yes, so long as that witness testifies. *People v. Rosario.* (New York, 1961.)

There were dozens.

Ventimiglia and whether a jury could hear about a defendant's uncharged, rather than *Molineux*'s past, crimes.

Huntley and whether a defendant's confession was given voluntarily.

Darden and whether a search warrant was justified.

Dawson and whether a surprise alibi witness was lying.

Sandoval and cross examining a defendant.

I scribbled the cases on legal pads, writing and rewriting their main points until they fit on a single sheet of paper that became my security blanket while sitting in waiting rooms. By the time I'd been selected for the panel interview with the Manhattan D.A.'s Office, the paper had become more important than my wallet.

"Make sure you go over your Professional Responsibility," Kyle advised. "Legal ethics was getting big when I was interviewing candidates. They'll probably pose a hypothetical. Don't give up. Answer the question and move on. It's actually pretty fun getting grilled by a bunch of prosecutors."

On the day of the panel, held in the Manhattan D.A.'s main office on the edge of Chinatown, I wore the same everything I had worn to my first interview with Ernie Mitchell. A dark blue, off the rack suit and a striped blue and gold tie from Brooks Brothers that a friend from New York had left at a wedding. I didn't own anything like it, and beyond the brand, the pattern struck me as big time.

When the door opened, three lawyers at the end of a large conference room stood and turned. Two men, Tim Dougherty and Abe Warren, and one woman, Sandy Terranova, introduced themselves. Without fanfare they began peppering me with questions.

"Tell us about yourself."

"Why do you want to work for this office?"

"Why prosecution?"

"Where else are you applying?"

"Why not defense work?"

"You're from Maryland, why New York?"

"What would you say are your strengths?"

"Why not Maryland?"

"Your weaknesses?"

After the first two minutes, I could feel myself bracing for the next question as I finished an answer. Sandy then threw on the brakes.

"You've just been hired by the office," she began.

"Congratulations," Abe smiled.

"Yes, congratulations," she continued. "You've just been hired by the office, and you're now on trial. The defendant is charged with raping a Radio City Rockette. You leave your office, and on the way to court you're suddenly surrounded by reporters. It's national news. 'Mr. Caulfield, Mr. Caulfield,' they say. They're looking for a quote. What do you do?"

Images of prosecutors giving stirring press conferences came to mind.

"No comment," I said.

"Why?" Sandy asked.

"First, the case is active and at a critical stage. Second, all things considered, more harm than good could come from me speaking spontaneously," I explained, slightly pleased with the stab at self-deprecation.

"OK," Sandy continued, unimpressed. "You pass by reporters, and just before you head inside, a court officer grabs you and says the hospital is on the phone. You take the call, and the doctor tells you the victim's just died. She was your only witness. You head into court, and before you can say anything, the defendant's attorney approaches and says his client will plead guilty.

He's changed his mind about a long drawn out trial and all of the media attention. Do you disclose?"

"Well, I would need to call a supervisor..."

"You can't," Tim intoned. "The judge called for a jury panel. You have no time."

Thinking...stalling...

"I'd ask to approach the bench," I said, "...and...without telling the judge or defense attorney, ask for a brief recess. 'Some matters not previously anticipated had just come up...'"

Sandy struck an annoyed tone. "Counsel, you've had this case for months. There will be no...more...delays. Not one more minute."

Tim looked at Sandy. "Judge Garrison?"

"And," Abe pitched in, "all modes of communication have just gone down."

Unsure where I would end up, I answered.

"If...without the witness...I can't prove my case...then... ethically... I'd have to disclose...that the witness died."

The answer felt right. Kyle would disagree later. Thankfully, the look on Sandy's face told me nothing.

She moved on.

"You pass by the reporters, and now a detective on the case comes up and says he has to tell you something. It's urgent. Five years ago he was investigated and then charged with perjury. It involved an investigation and an arrest he had made on a grocery store robbery. Do you disclose?"

I started to answer, but Abe spoke first.

"He was acquitted."

Tim chuckled, and with that I changed my answer, regretting it instantly.

"No," I said. "I wouldn't turn that over."

Abe pounced.

"Why not?"

"What bearing would it have on the detective's truthfulness?" I replied, trying to hold ground.

Tim openly laughed. "What *bearing* would it have on the detective's truthfulness?! He was charged with perjury!" He crossed his leg and slapped his shoe grinning at me and then Sandy and Abe.

I shifted in my seat and crossed my own leg, but the body language of it all made me wish I hadn't.

"OK, he was convicted," Sandy said. "Same answer?"

"No, I would turn that over."

"Assume it's now the defendant who was charged with perjury. Can you bring that out?" Sandy asked.

"He wasn't acquitted," Tim said.

For the first time I knew where they were going.

"Will the defendant testify?" I asked.

"Yes."

"It would depend on *Sandoval*," I answered, referring to the New York case where a judge must decide what parts of a defendant's criminal history a prosecutor could bring out.

When I answered, I happened to be looking at Sandy. She smiled slightly before looking away.

I got it, I thought, and it warmed me to the core.

"OK, but the case is on appeal," Tim said.

"Same answer," I said.

Abe leaned in.

"Back to the detective, the one acquitted. Just after telling you he was acquitted, he says that he actually *lied* on the stand."

I arched back and groaned, totally flat footed.

Bull's eye.

Abe laughed, delighted.

Six

GET OVER YOURSELF. SOMETIMES,
YOU HAVE TO FAKE IT

"May it please the court..."

I had been with the panel for just over thirty minutes by the time I left. Faced with their endless arsenal of *what ifs*, I opted for humor in answering Abe's question.

"I'd tell the attorney," I said about my lying detective, "but only after taking him out back..." It was the closest I could bring myself to saying, "I give in." Mentally, I was spent, but I didn't break a sweat. I hoped they appreciated that.

An hour and a half later, I was on Long Island standing in the October air outside the Nassau County D.A.'s Office, famished and tired. In another three hours, I would be farther east in Suffolk

County. The bright idea of scheduling three interviews spanning sixty miles after waking up at three-thirty in the morning to first travel two hundred miles wasn't looking so hot anymore.

My brain was mush. My heart also wasn't into it.

I gulped fall air and pep-talked my way inside. Despite the effort and my desire for a job, I was about to learn how difficult faking it was.

Nassau County was reportedly in the middle of a major financial crisis. In response, the D.A.'s Office there had scaled back staff and begun using junior prosecutors on an as-needed basis. It may have helped tame a flaming budget, but it was hell on recruiting.

The office was known to candidates for its hypothetical opening statement. A few weeks prior to the interview, each candidate received a standard set of "facts" and was expected to deliver a ten minute opening statement to an imaginary jury with a prosecutor from the hiring committee playing the part of judge.

Given the sky's-the-limit opportunity to test the mettle of young lawyers with imagined scenarios like the rape of a Radio City Rockette prosecuted under the klieg lights of national media frenzy, the Nassau D.A.'s Office chose to temper expectations. The single sheet of paper I received involved a midnight carjacking on a seventy-one mile stretch of cracked concrete known as the Long

Island Expressway, second only to the New Jersey Turnpike in east coast commuter ire.

Christine Brancaccio, the hiring attorney, walked me down a hall to a small abandoned office. After telling her the standard little bit about myself, I stood up to give my opening statement.

I may get out of this!, I thought as the interview juices began to flow. Two seconds into my opening, she stopped me.

"You forgot, 'May it please the court,'" she said.

With that the interview was all but over.

May it please the court.

If there were five words, the abuse of which typified the banal aspects of law school, the rigid, drink-the-Kool-Aid, I AM LAWYER, HEAR ME blah blah persona, they were, "May it please the court."

In a much different time and more rarefied place, "May it please the Court" (big C) meant something. A lawyer, surrounded by deep mahogany and brass railings, sat on a burgundy leather chair in an appellate court.

He or she would rise, buoyed by weeks, months and even years of preparation for this moment where there were no do overs.

"May it please the Court," he would say, and with that pay homage to the traditional and daunting task of asking a group of judges or, in the case of the U.S. Supreme Court, nine justices, to see *it* his way.

It had been decided before by a lesser court. But *it* still wasn't clear or settled law. So, those who wanted it a certain way hired serious lawyers to settle it their way. And vice versa. These lawyers saw appellate judges who listened to oral arguments.

But they weren't *arguments*. They were controlled burns, fueled by intellect and countless hours of planning. They appeared effortless as the lawyer-advocate advanced the cause despite calls by the judges for minute facts and parried, patient and unflappable, with precedents, prior case law, that had guided past courts.

In the summer of 1971, forty-six year old Alexander Bickel, a constitutional law juggernaut from Yale, convinced six members of the Supreme Court that *The New York Times* deserved First Amendment protection after publishing "The Pentagon Papers," the U.S. government's classified Vietnam strategy dating back to 1945.

Bickel began, "Mr. Chief Justice, may it please the Court."

Six months later, Sarah Weddington, a Texas lawyer, and twenty years Bickel's junior, convinced seven members of the

Court that young Norma L. McCorvey, better known as Jane Roe, had the right to privacy and an abortion.

Weddington, at twenty-six, was believed to have been the youngest person ever to win a United States Supreme Court case.

She began, "Mr. Chief Justice, and may it please the Court."

In 2000, I was the same age as Sarah Weddington when she opened in 1972.

May it please the Court?

I would have wet my pants.

It was those history making cases and the laws they defended (or struck down) why I went to law school. To get "there." To someday be considered a serious lawyer.

I couldn't prove it, but within the last decade or so some poor soul highjacked "May it please the Court" and began a forgettable lecture. Or welcomed an incoming class of first year law students. Or called to order some meeting. The intent, innocent enough, was to cast an ordinary event into something impressive and scholarly just because lawyers (or lawyers to be) were sitting there.

The consequence was that less serious lawyers kinda liked what they heard and spread it like a novice lawyer virus along with words and phrases I'd been hearing students spout like "glean"[1] and "beyond the pale."[2] Rather than being impressed, listeners came to expect something toothless and lame.

May it please the court...

...may I have a Coke?

Considering the popularity of lawyer jokes, I shouldn't have been surprised by antics like the misuse of "May it please the Court" when I got to law school and other inane acts like padding to exams in morning breath and pajamas, certain students much too busy to brush their teeth, shower or change. It cheapened an otherwise great experience.

Now, along with everything I had heard about the Nassau County D.A.'s Office, unfairly or not, Christine Brancaccio's call for "May it please the court" was now cheapening my view of becoming a prosecutor there. I couldn't shake it.

My opening statement, my entire interview, was toothless and lame. Whether it was Christine, the peanut butter and crackers crying out from my jacket to be opened and devoured or some

---

1   **glean** *verb* \'glēn\ – to gather grain left by reapers; to gather information bit by bit. As in, "In reading *Roe v. Wade,* I was able to glean..."

2   **beyond the pale** – unacceptable; outside common decency standards. "Pale" is an obsolete word meaning a stake or pointed piece of wood. To be "beyond the pale" was understood historically to mean outside of a fenced enclosure that protected the occupants, generally livestock.

cosmic force, it was all the same. As I left the office, I knew I'd never hear from them again. If I did, I pretty much knew what they were going to say.

This was one moment I couldn't do over.

Seven

CHOICES ARE A LUXURY

It'll Look Fabulous

I controlled nothing, and it was maddening. I wanted to work in the Manhattan D.A.'s Office and reached out to everyone, making as many connections as I could. I'd survived one interview and was waiting to hear if I'd survived the second. But as soon as October ended, Thanksgiving appeared, and all momentum with every prosecutor's office screeched to a halt.

Manhattan, Suffolk County and The Bronx prosecutors' offices were still alive. Having not heard from either Brooklyn (Kings County) or Westchester County drew obvious conclusions. I didn't need to see any pictures to know my fate in Nassau.

Getting to D.A.N.Y.

December was days away and with it Christmas, a new year and the likelihood that I'd enter my final semester without a job. Married not even a year and with a child on the way, the pressure became immense. Feeling a bit unfaithful and a large bit desperate, I applied to law firms big and small across Long Island.

The response was mortifying. Each crisp sheet of linen, startlingly brief. After thanking me for my interest, the letters concluded:

> *Though your credentials are admirable, we regret to inform you that we are not hiring at this time.*

Eighteen words standing beside an open mailbox had never made me feel so worthless.

A morbid, pack-rat sense kicked in to distract from the growing desperation. To each letter, I stapled a copy of the cover letter and résumé I had submitted weeks earlier while images of law firm life drowned out the silence of the prosecutors. Rather than accomplish anything, in short order I had a cardboard box filled with rejections, filed alphabetically.

"Don't worry," Kyle said, hearing my voice the Monday after Thanksgiving.

"This is the big one, the third interview. Most people get the second. Most don't get the third. Give it a few more days. They've got a lot of candidates."

The next day, one of my professors, Father Hanlon, called me into his office and offered a way out, a clerkship with a district court judge in D.C.

I was surprised how my world opened. Far from jumping at it though, I kitten-ball-of-yarned it.

Helloooo, what do we have here?

[approach]…[sloooow]…[ciiirrcle]…[pawbackaway]… [paaw]… [pawpaw]…

[pawPawPAW!PAW!PAW!]

Father watched me play.

"Father has sent a lot of graduates her way," Father Hanlon said, referring to himself in the third person, a habit his students found amusing. "Her" was Judge Karen Susanan, Father's close friend.

"It'll look fabulous on your résumé."

Yarn was everywhere.

"I can't have you back out," he said, halting my thoughts of a clerkship safety net.

"Last year, Father recommended a student, and the student promised Father he was interested. But he wasn't being truthful with Father. That made Father very angry."

Guilt ridden, I confessed to Father, who proceeded to belittle Paul.

"You don't want a private firm on Long Island," he said. "You'll never make any money. You'll work hard, but you'll never be happy."

"To be honest, I want to prosecute," I said.

"Why would you want to do that? You'll never make any money there either," said the Catholic priest.

"I like the idea of prosecuting. Trying cases. Helping people."

"That's what *pro bono*'s for!" Father exclaimed, referring to free work attorneys are encouraged to do each year.

He went on laying waste to the idea of public service as a profession.

"How are you going to buy a house and care for your children?"

I told him that I liked criminal over civil law.

"Where are you going to go after?"

I had no answer, so he continued.

"What skills are you going to get there?"

I had no interest in answering, so he finished.

"You know I can't push for you."

I knew that, shook his hand and left. As I did, three emotions washed over me. Embarrassment, surprise and anger. The first one caused the other two.

Eight

At moments of truth, be yourself

She Spoke No Verb

The look of concern on Alyssa's face was unsettling when I told her that night. We were in a booth of a Georgetown pub having drinks with one of my brothers. Our friend Jerry and his wife were meeting us. When they walked in, my brother went over. That's when I turned to Alyssa and told her about Father.

I thought she'd take it differently, *We're in this together! New York or bust!* But, without saying a word (my brother, Jerry and his wife were now sliding into our booth), we agreed. This could be a huge bust.

Jerry, a lawyer, added his own two cents an hour later.

"I don't think you'll get it," he said matter-of-factly.

Seeing my face drop, he softened. "It's a hard job to get. I didn't get it."

Later, I wrote it off as Jerry being Jerry. Having known him for years, though, it still hurt and added to a rough few days.

Thankfully, the letter came, and with it Jerry's prediction delayed. I would meet Michelle Dylan, Chief of Legal Hiring for the Manhattan D.A.'s Office on Tuesday morning, December 5, 2000.

If the line I'd heard held true, this, not any later meeting with Morgenthau, the D.A. himself, was the crucial interview. She either liked you or she didn't. As gatekeeper to the office, she'd be damned to pass you along if she didn't.

"Mention my name," Kyle said later, sounding enthusiastic.

"Really?"

"I used to do on campus interviews for her. She'll know who I am. We got along great."

I had no idea how I'd name drop in a no-fat interview and walk away unscathed.

"Does she ask any hypos?" I asked. I hoped not, six weeks removed but still raw from the panel.

"No. She just wants to make sure you're good for the office. They teach you the law."

They teach me the law. So good!

Five days later I was in New York, specifically the ninth floor bathroom of 1 Hogan Place. I didn't have to go, but I couldn't stand sitting in the waiting room. In the history of interviewing, there is no worse feeling than seeing "the guy before you" come out of his interview with a smile on his face or in a remotely good mood.

It was the second time I had taken refuge in that bathroom, that stall to be exact, the panel having taken place a few rooms away. Lieutenant Richie Callahan stilled sucked, as someone had written in black marker on the stall's door. But someone in blue had since clarified the sentiment, adding a male appendage (and an exclamation point).

It was comforting, the empty bathroom. Me there in my own private green room. If only someone would now peak their head in, *Mr. Caulfield, you're on*, I'd stay there with Richie until they called my number.

"Come in," Michelle Dylan said fifteen minutes later.

Her office was narrow, a desk at the far end with a single, standard issue metal chair in front. Stanley Kubrick had done doctors' offices. Medical exams on stainless steel under hot lights and by expressionless doctors bathed in white. Had the exam room been windowed, it would have opened to an ice planet.

Michelle Dylan's was the next building over.

She would ask just four questions.

"Paul, have a seat."

She did not get up.

I sat down.

"So, why here?"

The absence of a verb was devastating in probing efficiency. Candidates had answered that question dozens, if not hundreds, of times before sitting in that chair. They had an answer, and she knew it.

I had been asked that question by Kyle Miller, Ernie Mitchell, the panel, Father Hanlon, my wife and myself countless of times and its kissing cousins in Nassau, The Bronx (twice) and Suffolk County (three times).

Getting to D.A.N.Y.

Michelle Dylan wasn't interested in the answer. She wanted to see if it came out sounding like, "Welcome to McDonald's. May I take your order?"

I lumbered through finishing stronger than I started.

Question two came on its heels.

"What bureau do you see yourself in?"

There were three possible assignments for new hires, and I ticked off each of them – a Trial Bureau, the Appeals Division and the Office of Special Narcotics.

I liked them in that order, I said, throwing a curve with Appeals, reportedly more of a third choice among candidates. Few wanted to just research and write. Most wanted to investigate and try cases. Trial Bureaus and Special Narcotics offered just that.

Taking the lion's share of "rookies" were six Trial Bureaus, numbered 30 through 80, each with an average of forty Assistant D.A.s made up of a bureau chief, two deputies, one or two senior trial counsel, felony and junior line assistants and eight or so rookies. Each outfit picked up arrests according to a rotating six-day schedule with more senior prosecutors also developing cases through cop connections and homegrown investigations.

Misdemeanors were randomly assigned to rookies and second years after arrest processing, or intake, by another assistant, generally a rookie. Ambiguously defined though worthy second years and senior attorneys prosecuted felony cases "vertically," from intake through disposition. While these assistants ate what they killed, a supervisor was on hand to ensure budding felony assistants didn't bite off more than they could chew. Homicides, for example, went to homicide assistants, those who had passed a clearer threshold and worked the Homicide Chart, trial bureau Shangri-La.

Twenty-four hour cycles were broken into three shifts: day, night and "lobster," the last one due to the high probability that fishermen on the high seas were the only other laborers awake.

If rookies and junior assistants weren't on intake, they were manning one of those shifts arraigning cases, staffing status hearings or at their desks working a mushrooming caseload and at-the-ready if called for trial.

Senior attorneys, having graduated from prosecuting a few hundred active defendants, were at their desks, in the field or with grand juries managing an enviable few to few dozen cases. In the context of war, trial bureau work was front line stuff…being a rookie, in *the shit*.

There was just one Appeals Bureau, hands down the most civilized of assignments. With its steady, nine-to-five work week, manageable caseloads and business casual attire, the Bureau, as its name bespoke, was legal research and brief writing conducted in the confines of one's office. Every so often, it culminated in the most thrilling aspect of the job, if not the entire office – standing before the New York Court of Appeals and uttering the true sense of "May it please the Court," ready to draw fire in the name of the Manhattan District Attorney.

Of the four or five rookies assigned to Appeals each year, not everyone wanted the assignment. The Appeals Bureau may have meant a stable existence and the chance, albeit infrequently, to sing soprano at The Met, but it was mostly viewed as a staid assignment compared to its gnarly counterparts.

If there was a rock star, it was the Office of the Special Narcotics Prosecutor. It dazzled candidates, beginning with its nickname, "Spec Narc," and unique though brief history. Created in response to an exploding heroin craze in the summer of 1971, the city's five then-elected district attorneys gave it life on February 3, 1972. On that day, they abdicated a bit of their local powers and offered a few of their assistants to centralize the prosecution of major drug offenses under Frank J. Rogers, New York City's first Special Narcotics Prosecutor. He was thirty-eight years old and, until that time, a career assistant with the Manhattan D.A.'s Office.

A palpable feel emerged as Spec Narc made a name for itself and it and D.A.N.Y. became the big kids on the prosecutors' block. It began with Frank Rogers, one of Manhattan's own, but there was something more.

By 2000, Spec Narc's headquarters and that of the Manhattan D.A. sat side by side at 80 and 100 Centre Street just north of the Manhattan side of the Brooklyn Bridge. It didn't hurt that another Manhattan Assistant D.A., Bridget Brennan, had since taken the lead at Spec Narc. In doing so she set another favorable distinction, becoming the first woman to hold the position now widely accepted as the city's sixth District Attorney.

Above all else, Spec Narc's most alluring aspect was this – as many as eight rookies entered Spec Narc as felony assistants and bypassed eighteen months of slogging it out with petty thieves and minor aggressors as misdemeanor prosecutors. At Spec Narc, they'd work confidential informants, search warrants and wire taps to tackle narcotics enterprises on the local, national and international scale dealing in heroin, cocaine and the newest epidemic, designer drugs ecstasy and ketamine.

Heady stuff for any young lawyer who dreamed of working with undercover cops in hoodies and three day stubble doing "no-knock entries," otherwise known as BREAKTHEGODDAMNDOORDOWN! with a ram, a literal battering ram, in cracked out dens.

Despite the allure, I said as I finished my assessment, I was unsure about a typecasting element in Spec Narc. Trial

Bureaus and Appeals offered vastly different lifestyles. For the former, street and white collar crimes, domestic violence and child abuse on the front lines of trial work. For the latter, the epitome of "they teach you the law." Either one was where I saw myself.

"Have you had any experience with either?" Dylan replied, her third question in now ten minutes.

"Well, I tried about a dozen cases with a county prosecutor and am doing a fair amount of research and writing in D.C."

"That's not what I meant," she said. "I meant domestic violence and child abuse. You mentioned them."

I hadn't seen one of those cases and was about to say so. Instead, I'd tie my response to a new marriage and an expecting wife to explain a greater appreciation for spouses and children. Not much, but it would have to do.

Then I remembered Ecuador.

With that, a flood of memories washed over me. One, in particular. I began to speak, and when I did, a separate thought popped into my head.

If you get this job, it's because of what you're about to say.

One night, the other volunteers and I had just finished dinner. We could hear everything coming from the homes up and down the dirt streets.

Shouting was common, so when we heard it, no one said anything. It got louder, starting with a man's voice and then a woman's, followed by crashes, more voices and people running to our neighbor's two room shack.

Victoria Elena.

Vicki.

Hola, Veeki.

Vicki had two daughters and worked in the daycare on the first floor of our volunteer house. She stood out as much for her quiet nature and calm delivery, *Hola, Pablito*, as she did for her striking good looks.

Someone knocked at our door.

Nick, another volunteer, and I ran downstairs.

"They're calling for you," a teenager said.

Our hearts pounding, we sprinted next door, stopping at the uneven, slatted stairs that led up to Vicki's house. The door was open, and the front room brightly lit. Vicki's younger daughter was just outside, her older one in the doorway. A man we had never seen before was in the back of the house with Vicki a foot or so away.

"He won't leave!" she said, seeing us. She was upset, an emotion I'd never seen from her.

Nick walked in. I stayed with the girls.

"Who is he?" I asked, turning to a neighbor.

"Her husband. He's drunk."

We'd lived in Durán for six months. I'd never seen Vicki standing near a man. Not once had it occurred to me that she was married.

"It's my house," drunk husband called out, his words a wreck.

Vicki moved to push him. "I want him out! He's never around, and now he wants to be with me."

It was clear what she meant, her hair and clothes a mess, and he, without a shirt, leaning, pointing, toward her.

Nick moved toward him. One of my closest friends from college, Nick thrived in dusts ups and tight spots.

"Let's go outside," Nick said to drunk husband, more pronouncement than request, draping a heavy arm around drunk husband's shoulder. In doing so, Nick now stood between drunk husband and Vicki.

"It's my house," drunk husband repeated, ignoring us. The wreak of booze was everywhere. Except his breath. That was a separate assault.

"Come back tomorrow," Nick said sweetly, his face close to drunk husband's. I'd known Nick for years and knew what he was thinking. His pleasant smile said it all.

Drunk husband, I will punch your lights out if you try anything.

Drunk husband, nestled in Nick's thick frame, moped to the front, mumbling the incomprehensible. In the ten feet it took to get drunk husband outside, it was over.

Vicki began pulling herself together and called for her daughters. Outside, drunk husband made a half-hearted attempt to head back in before finally stumbling off.

The next day and the day after, he returned. A matter of pride to show that he could. By the third day he was gone. Soon after, Vicki went back to being Vicki.

I finished speaking and hoped Michelle Dylan would ask a question about Ecuador. She didn't. She asked her final question, *Where did I see myself in five years?*

"I'd like to be here," I said. Running into her on my way to court.

Cheesy but true.

The interview ended.

Before rising to leave, I took a shot at making a deeper impression.

"Kyle Miller asked that I say hello."

The words were stilted despite having just spoken for fifteen minutes.

She reacted. Barely.

"Oh, Kyle, he was a very good assistant. We were sorry to see him go. Pay hello to him for me."

That was it.

Four questions, three verbs and a "pay hello." Not what I expected. During the entire time we were together, Michelle Dylan spoke for a total of thirty seconds. If she wanted material to judge, she had it in spades. The interview might as well have been a screen test.

It was then that I left my third interview with the Manhattan D.A.'s Office, the process all but over. I would either see the Boss or get a rejection.

But as I left, something was new.

I had a smile on my face and was in a remotely good mood.[3]

---

3 As *Getting to D.A.N.Y.* neared publication, the interviewing prosecutor referred to as Michelle Dylan was kind enough to revisit her vetting process. "I really wanted to understand what motivated applicants and wanted them to talk about their dreams and experiences and their reactions to their experiences." She added that she applied, to all candidates, "a full résumé review…designed to test integrity, sense of justice and ability to think." One of her points was that her interviews were more thorough than depicted here. I've kept the original text unchanged, however, particularly due to the efficient nature of the interview and how it felt for me, the candidate.

Nine

When you're wrong, admit it

Nasty

The good mood lasted about twelve hours. I then became a total jerk. All because of a misplaced phone call.

"Why are you being so nasty?" Alyssa asked the night after the interview.

To celebrate D.A.N.Y. looking up, she had cooked salmon. It, a bottle of wine and steaming couscous sat on the kitchen table. I had just said something terrible about one of them. Probably the salmon.

She stood by the stove waiting for an answer.

I didn't have a clue.

All I knew was that after a short-lived euphoria, a deep funk set in, and my wife was now bearing the brunt of it.

A rational voice sounded off in the haze…

She didn't deserve that. Say it — "I'm sorry."

… followed by a much bigger and way more irrational thought…

Forget that. Say something nastier. Maybe she'll go away.

I chose to say nothing, slouching in my chair, poking at bits of fish and eating none of it. Alyssa walked out of the room and then upstairs, her own plate of food sitting untouched next to mine.

After a few minutes, I could hear her in bed. Four months pregnant with our first child. But alone.

Why are you doing this?

A short time ago, I wanted to be a hometown lawyer. Now all I could think about was something completely different. Not just a job but a standard I had created. A standard I had taken for granted and hadn't given a moment's pause.

I was paused now, boy, and what I saw was frightening.

Getting to D.A.N.Y.

I wasn't all that great.

For his part, Father Hanlon questioned that standard, and it riled me to no end. At least he saw something, enough to propose a D.C. clerkship. A steadier and certainly less cockier hand may have taken it. I didn't, opting instead to go all-chips-in on another game, thinking that wanting something bad enough was somehow good enough.

My friend Jerry had mostly mocked my chances and, intentionally or not, took a wrecking ball to my spirits. While it also amped my desire to *show him!*, there was no escaping it. Jerry Fellows personified the shame I'd feel if I didn't get the job.

The Brooklyn and Westchester D.A.s' Offices sure hadn't seen much in me. I still hadn't heard from either. Long Island law firms unanimously agreed. While the Bronx prosecutor's office remained a strong possibility and, as of that morning, Suffolk County a lock, getting either had become second place. In some warped way, I'd rather have neither if Manhattan didn't pan out, preferring an unknown bronze to silver. To be thirty minutes late for the plane, God, please not thirty *seconds*.

In moments like these, Kyle Miller had been a phone call away to offer counsel and calm. As of that morning, his advice seemingly failed for the first time.

"Suffolk County called," I explained. "They'd like me to meet the D.A. I think I got the job."

"When?" Kyle asked.

"Next week," I said. "Friday."

I'd never hear back from Manhattan by then, and similar to Manhattan, if offered the job, Suffolk County's District Attorney, James Catterson, expected you to accept.

"Call them," Kyle said.

"Who?"

"Manhattan. Legal Hiring. Tell them you just met with Michelle and that you've now received an invitation to meet with Catterson for the Suffolk job on Friday. Tell them you'll be up the day before. They'll get it."

"You want me to call Legal Hiring?" The word *hardball* popped into my head.

"Yes."

I called Legal Hiring.

When I hung up, I was sick. I imagined "Joan" walking down the hall to Michelle Dylan's office forcing the issue, certain it would ruin my chances.

Joan's promised call back didn't come. As the day ended, I was beside myself. Now it was dinner, and dinner was ruined. My wife laid out upstairs, an innocent bystander.

She didn't deserve that.

I know.

I had known my wife for eight years. We began as friends in college. If there was such a thing as an "in" crowd, she'd been part of it. More than that and what struck me as utterly unique was her ability to move between crowds one day and go off by herself the next. She made the math club look cool.

Just before winter break my sophomore year, I saw her standing alone in the campus center when it hit me. She was wearing a bright orange jacket that had become her trademark around campus. Fit for a deer hunter but made more ironic and thereby cute because she didn't eat meat.

Mario Puzo, author of *The Godfather*, described the moment when Michael Corleone, hiding out in Sicily, first laid eyes on Apollonia.

All the perfumes of the island came rushing in on the wind, orange, lemon blossoms, grapes, flowers. It seemed as if his body had sprung away from him out of himself.

Hyperbole aside, I'd never forget where I was standing when I saw Alyssa Pentoney that December afternoon. Thankfully, she wouldn't die in a car bomb on page 350.

Fifteen months later, we started dating. When we did, a few friends who knew how crazy I was about her sought me out and congratulated me, a nod to the time and effort it took to get my college-boy act together and show her I was serious.

Three years later, I proposed. Now, it was another December, and we were a month away from our first anniversary. Five months from a child.

The cliché in break-ups is, *It's not you, it's me.* Alyssa and I weren't breaking up, and this wasn't a cliché – it absolutely was me, not her. She could have had Emeril Lagasse slave over steak tartare, stuffed lobster and garlic mashers. I still would have said something petty about dinner. All in the off chance that putting her down would somehow lift me up.

Somewhere within the last few weeks, I'd become a therapist's dream.

I got up from the table and went upstairs. Still awake, she had her knees pulled up, and her hair lay across her face. The sight spoke louder and pierced deeper than any *Why are you being so nasty?* It merged with who she was and became what we had before rotting into how I'd acted. If one emotion could ever dial into the senses, it was then.

At the clickety-clack peak of a roller coaster, there was exhilaration. Grief at the sudden loss of another. Standing in our bedroom, I was sorry.

I said it.

When she didn't move, I said it again, now sitting on the bed.

"Why are you so worried?" she said quietly, not moving, her back to me.

"I shouldn't have called there."

She rolled over.

"You've got the job with Suffolk County. What's wrong with that?"

"Nothing."

All along I could have just talked to her like this.

"I don't think it was a mistake," she said. "What would you do if you just waited? Would you take Suffolk County?"

She was now lightly rubbing my arm.

"I would have to."

"Wouldn't you feel worse if you then got the interview with Manhattan?"

I didn't answer. After a while, she fell asleep. A while later, so did I.

We were well on the mend by the next night. When I got home, Alyssa was sitting on the couch.

"I think there's a message for you," she said, paying more attention to the TV.

"Manhattan?" I asked hopefully, throwing my stuff by the door.

"I don't know," she said, distracted. "I skipped it when I heard it was for you."

I dialed and listened.

"Yes, this message is for Paul Caulfield. This is Ida Van Lindt from Mr. Morgenthau's office. He would like to meet with you next week. Please call me to schedule an appointment."

Ida Van Lindt was Morgenthau's personal secretary. She'd been at the office for decades, having worked for Morgenthau's predecessor, Frank Hogan.

"I came with the building," she once wise-cracked to a reporter.

Unless I botched it with either Ida or Morgenthau that next week, I very likely had the job. I was shaking when I hung up the phone and turned around. Alyssa had quietly come up from behind.

Her face said it all. She already knew.

"Yeah, Paulie!" she shouted, a broad smile on her face.

She'd been behind me all along.

Ten

Part One: Not Happy Birthday

Ida Van Lindt confirmed I'd meet Morgenthau the next week. Thursday, December 14, 2000. The day before my final interview with Suffolk County.

Kyle Miller assured me the hardest part was over.

"Congratulations. Go in, speak with Mr. Morgenthau, and if he makes you an offer, accept. After that, call Suffolk County."

My brother congratulated me, as well.

"Dude, you must have interviewed your ass off."

Getting to D.A.N.Y.

I laughed and thought of Kyle.

The entire vibe of the job hunt changed after Ida's call. A few nights before the final interview with Mr. Morgenthau, I was on my computer savoring the laziness of poking around the internet. Absentmindedly, I went to the Manhattan D.A.'s website.

I'd read for months on its *History* page how the office claimed 1935 as the year of its modern-day birth. With Thomas E. Dewey's appointment as special prosecutor, the next sixty-five years included Dewey officially taking the job in 1938 before moving on to the governor's mansion and presidential politics. Frank S. Hogan followed in 1942 and registered thirty-two years before leaving in poor health in 1974. After an interim stint by Richard Kuh, Morgenthau took office in January 1975. Twenty-five years later, he was still prosecuting.[4]

A mural I'd seen twice at the 1 Hogan Place headquarters reinforced this history. Black-and-white photographs and grainy headlines covered a wall outside the executive offices. From floor to ceiling were the decades of Dewey, Hogan and Morgenthau. Typed alongside the courthouse candids, press conferences and mug shots were three words:

Prosecution, not politics.

---

4 Robert Morgenthau would remain in office for a record thirty-four years, retiring in December 2009 at the age of 90.

But for all of the mural's *Here be crime fighters!* bent, what about before 1935? By then, the District Attorney's Office was over a hundred years old. There were earlier D.A.s, of course; I just hadn't heard of them.

With little to base it on, I assumed that those years and decades were intentionally forgotten, embarrassment tied to Tammany Hall. Any pre-1935 mural would have glorified that century-plus political machine, a paean to gorging politicians and toothless law enforcement. Absent in any D.A. mural of the Tammany Hall days would have been the increasingly disenfranchised – minorities, women and the poor.

Politics. Not prosecution.

Then I began researching it.

Thirty-seven men, I discovered, preceded Thomas Dewey, beginning with D.A. Richard Riker in 1801.[5] Rather than being elected, he and the initial D.A.s were selected by the New York Council of Appointment and then, in 1821, by the Court of General Sessions. Only in 1846, did the state's constitution call for a popular vote, which went to D.A. John McKeon.[6]

---

5 Before 1801, the New York Attorney General prosecuted crimes in what is now New York County.

6 D.A. years: 1846 – 1850 and 1882 – 1883.

These early D.A.s occupied the office for as brief as *eight* days[7] and as long as eleven years.[8] Five D.A.s, including Riker and McKeon, returned to office twice.[9] More than a few served less than a year, while handfuls completed full terms of three and, later, four years. The most volatile year, 1883, saw four men in the D.A.'s chair with three cycling in and out between Thanksgiving and Christmas.

Their experiences were as predictable as they were eclectic. Many went to Columbia for college, law or both. Riker and D.A. Barent Gardenier[10] were wounded in duels (separately). A few were soldiers in the War of 1812. Of those who later served the Union, D.A. John Fellows[11] served time…but as a Confederate prisoner.

D.A. John Rodman translated and published France's Commercial Code.[12] D.A.s N. Bowditch Blunt and his brother Joseph almost served consecutive terms.[13] D.A. Vernon Davis taught Greek, mathematics and logic.[14] D.A. A. Oakey Hall was a New Orleans journalist and the author of a hit Christmas song of

---

7 John Vincent in 1883.

8 Richard Riker, D.A. years: 1801 – 1810 and 1811 – 1813.

9 Riker; Hugh Maxwell, 1817 – 1818 and 1821 – 1829; McKeon; A. Oakey Hall, 1855 – 1857 and 1862 – 1868; and John R. Fellows, 1888 – 1890 and 1894 – 1896.

10 D.A. years: 1813 – 1815.

11 D.A. years: 1888 – 1890.

12 D.A. years: 1815 – 1817.

13 D.A. years: 1851 – 1854 and 1858, respectively.

14 D.A. year: 1896.

his time, "Old Whitey's Christmas Trot."[15] After a storied, though colorful career, Hall suffered a nervous breakdown and retired to London.

D.A. William Jerome[16] was cousins with Winston Churchill.

Unsurprisingly, they came from local and state politics. They became U.S. congressmen and senators. Presidents nominated them for positions domestic and abroad.

Presidents James Monroe and Zachary Taylor appointed D.A.s Rodman and Hugh Maxwell Collectors of Ports in Florida and New York, respectively. President James K. Polk installed D.A. Lorenzo Shepard[17] as one of New York's federal prosecutors. President Franklin Pierce did the same for McKeon, and for D.A. Samuel Garvin,[18] he made federal prosecutor for North Dakota.

President Millard Fillmore offered D.A. (Joseph) Blunt the role of Commissioner to China, but Blunt declined. President Grover Cleveland nominated D.A. Wheeler Peckham[19] to the U.S. Supreme Court, but Peckham was unsuccessful. President Theodore Roosevelt appointed D.A. Eugene Philbin[20] to investigate deteriorating conditions on Ellis Island.

---

15 D.A. years: 1855 – 1857 and 1862 – 1868.
16 D.A. years: 1902 – 1909.
17 D.A. year: 1854.
18 D.A. years: 1869 – 1872.
19 D.A. year: 1883.
20 D.A. years: 1900 – 1901.

Of the sensational cases, there were plenty. New York society was atwitter in the spring of 1836 when D.A. Thomas Phoenix[21] prosecuted Richard Robinson for killing Helen Jewett with a hatchet. Robinson was nineteen years old and of moderate privilege, Jewett a prostitute to the upper class.

Phoenix's jury failed to sympathize with his victim and her choice of profession and sided with the defendant and his choice of attorney, former D.A. Ogden Hoffman[22]…Phoenix's predecessor.

Six years later, another jury agreed with D.A. James Whiting[23] after his defendant, John Colt, took his own hatchet and killed a local printer. The New York press dutifully reported Colt's penchant for gambling and women as well as his connections with brother Samuel of Colt Revolver fame. The pinnacle moment came not when the foreman read, "Guilty," but after, when Colt plunged a knife into his chest on the day of his hanging, thus avoiding execution.

With the rise of the news rag there was, of course, the "Trial of the Century." In 1907, D.A. William Jerome prosecuted playboy Harry Kendall Thaw for murdering architect Stanford White, renowned for many designs including New York's Washington Square Arch.

---

21 D.A. years: 1835 – 1838.

22 D.A. years: 1829 – 1835.

23 D.A. years: 1838 – 1844.

The case had all the markings for Hollywood. Thaw was heir to an oil and rail fortune. He was also wildly jealous of White, who years earlier had bedded model and former "It Girl" Evelyn Nesbitt, Thaw's new wife. Thaw shot White after a chance encounter on the rooftop of Madison Square Garden, another of White's creations.

After a three month trial, D.A. Jerome's closing argument ended with a theatrical flourish:

"And since my learned opponent has seen fit to go to the Scriptures for words that might guide you [the jury], let me, too, call your attention to two things that stand written as of old –

'Vengeance is mine, saith the Lord. I shall repay.'

And the other that came from amid the thunders of Sinai and which has embodied in the code of every civilized race for thousands of years.

'Thou shalt not kill.'"[24]

Yet, for D.A.s like Jerome, there were plenty who reinforced my presumption of a prosecutor's office in lockstep with Tammany

---

24 The jury deadlocked. A year later, a second jury found Thaw not guilty by reason of insanity and sentenced him to life in a state hospital. A third jury disagreed in 1915 and set him free. Thaw died of a heart attack in Miami, Florida in 1947. With that, Hollywood bit, and in 1955, twenty-two year old Joan Collins played the part of Nesbit in *The Girl on the Red Velvet Swing*. The film's title came from the titillating eccentricity White hung inside his midtown apartment.

Hall. Three served as Grand Sachems, Tammany Hall's highest honor: D.A.s Lorenzo Shepard, Nelson Waterbury[25] and Thomas Crain.[26] Other D.A.s were more notorious.

D.A. Oakey Hall "was bound for the highest stations of governor and even president," his obituary noted on October 8, 1898, "but for a strange flaw in his character, which led him often to do the opposite to that which he had apparently so elaborately planned." That flaw included associating with his first successor D.A. Peter B. Sweeny[27] and Tammany lord William "Boss" Tweed.

"$weeny," as then-popular cartoonist Thomas Nast dubbed him in *Harper's Weekly,* was considered the brains behind Tweed's legendary plundering of New York City.[28] Sweeny would twice be indicted for stealing while parks commissioner.

But D.A.s like Hugh Maxwell and Benjamin Phelps[29] shattered the façade that the early D.A.s were all like Sweeny and Hall.

A Columbia grad and Army JAG veteran, Maxwell pursued Tammany Hall during the 1820s, scoring convictions for the millions of dollars taken from banks, insurance companies and

---

25 D.A. years: 1859 – 1861.

26 D.A. years: 1930 – 1934.

27 D.A. year: 1858.

28 The trio of "Sweed, Tweeny & Co." enjoyed the full brunt of Nast's skewering caricatures in the early 1870s. Accompanying captions like "Tweedledee and Sweedledum," they found themselves reduced to pencil and ink, which succeeded in raising the nation's consciousness and hastened their exit from politics.

29 D.A. years: 1873 – 1880.

public at large. Unlike duelers Riker and Gardenier, Maxwell declined when challenged to a gun fight; unsurprisingly, it came from a Tammany man.

Fifty years later, D.A. Phelps added to this counterbalance, building an office worthy of the men who'd occupy it in the 20th Century. He surrounded himself with loyal staff who pursued criminals "with a vigor and determination that speedily made itself felt." On the night Phelps died, his former law partner, Vice President-elect Chester A. Arthur, sat by his bedside.

Phelps' 1880 obituary would have fit nicely alongside the mural of his next century successors:

A Bright Career Ended. Death of District Attorney Benjamin K. Phelps. A Leading Lawyer and a Successful Prosecutor.

...Mr. Phelps's accession to office marked a new era in the history of that most important branch of the City Government.

Under the regime of his Tammany predecessors, star chamber proceedings were the order of the day. The District Attorney – unless the applicant were some politician who had a pull in his district – was inaccessible to ordinary visitors, and citizens in quest of information found their entrance to the sanctum of the prosecuting officer of the county barred by impassable partitions and surly attendants.

Getting to D.A.N.Y.

Mr. Phelps signaled his accession to office by removing half a dozen ante-rooms and throwing the doors of every office in his department open to the humblest applicant. He received every visitor, no matter how poor or uninfluential, with courtesy, and patiently investigated every case brought to his notice. Thus it was that he became so popular with all classes of citizens, <u>irrespective of politics</u>.

The New York Times
December 31, 1880
(Emphasis added.)

Maxwell and Phelps were hardly alone,[30] but criminal justice and good government did ebb and flow. At the turn of the 20th Century, D.A. Asa Bird Gardiner cried, "the hell with reform!" in December 1900 and refused to prosecute anyone associated with Tammany Hall. For this defiance, then-Governor Roosevelt removed Gardiner from office.[31]

Two weeks later, another D.A. summed up the city's predicament and the magnitude of the remedy. At a dinner titled,

---

30 Randolph Martine (D.A. years: 1885 – 1887), a former Tammany member, took on corruption and graft. William Jerome, aside from his trial of the century, fought political corruption and was twice elected D.A. for it. Charles Whitman (D.A. years: 1910 – 1914) established night court and tackled election fraud before becoming D.A. His near unanimous re-election in 1913 was credited to his zeal for fairness and transparency that would vault him to the governor's chair the following year.

31 In a separate act of defiance, Gardiner, a Medal of Honor winner during the American Civil War, refused to return it after it was rescinded for the lack of corroboration.

"The Causes of Our Present Municipal Degradation," Democrats and Republicans listened to social reformers like Mark Twain rail against corruption and "the lust for gain and dishonesty." Presiding over the evening was one of shortest-tenured D.A.s who had become a well-respected lawyer of his time, Wheeler H. Peckham.

By that day, January 4, 1901, Peckham was unabashedly anti-Tammany Hall. As special prosecutor, he had pursued both Oakey Hall and Boss Tweed. Representing New York, he'd won a whopping six million dollar verdict against Tweed for fraud. A prominent constitutional lawyer and former Supreme Court nominee, when Peckham rose to deliver his introductory remarks, his audience must have leaned in.

Peckham placed blame squarely on the "bad, wholly and ir-redeemably bad" elected officials and recognized, as *The New York Times* recounted the next day:

> *"...that no man strong enough had yet come to the fore who could oust them and change matters. Men with the determination and morality to put out the wrongdoers and to put in others who would see that the misrule should cease had not yet shown themselves."*

Peckham continued:

> *"I tell you, my brothers, that it does not make a copper's difference whom you put in or whom you put out. No one man*

can create a force loyal to duty unless behind that man or that Commissioner there is the pressing force of public opinion which makes him feel that his position would be intolerable unless he did what was right. Organization, coordination of forces, these are the things that are most needed, and it is along these lines that the victory must lie."

Thirty-four years later, that pressing force of public opinion arrived. It came in the form a Manhattan grand jury and empowered the man on whom the Manhattan D.A.'s Office would later date its birth.

Part Two: Happy Birthday[32]

On a fall morning in 1935, Manhattan's newly appointed special prosecutor should have been lying in a pool of blood in an Upper East Side pharmacy, his breakfast still warm on the counter. He wasn't, for across the Hudson River in a Newark, New Jersey morgue, another body lay cold, twelve hours dead and the victim of a gangland murder.

The dead man, Arthur Flegenheimer, was better known as the gangster Dutch Schultz. He would never extort, bootleg or kill again. The special prosecutor, Thomas E. Dewey, finished his meal and headed to his office downtown, unaware of his good fortune.

---

32 "Happy Birthday" draws extensively (including direct quotations) from Richard Norton Smith's fantastic biography, *Thomas E. Dewey and His Times* (Simon & Schuster, 1982). Portions of independent research are woven throughout.

If the Manhattan D.A.'s Office calls 1935 the year of its modern-day birth, October 25th was the day...and former D.A. Peckham's foretelling of the events leading up to it, unmistakable.

Prohibition, despite its repeal in 1933, had created a vacuum that a fledgling New York mafia moved into before infecting entire industries. They exploited construction, trucking, sanitation, restaurants, nightclubs, the garment business, jewelry, railways and waterfronts. They created black markets in alcohol, drugs, gambling, fenced goods and protection and succeeded so entirely because they paid off or killed those who could have stopped them.

But while corruption's five-hundred million dollar wet blanket suffocated the city, by the spring of 1935, the Depression had mercifully bottomed out.[33] Recovery was underway, and New York's emboldened spirit was palpable.[34]

William Copeland Dodge, the newly elected District Attorney, must have sensed the changes around him and a very real opportunity for his office. Being openly pro-Tammany Hall,

---

33 Between 1932 and 1933, unemployment hit twenty-five percent, which accounted for thirteen million people out of work. Average household incomes dropped forty percent, and the federal government counted more than sixty percent of all Americans as poor. Eleven thousand banks, almost forty-five percent of all U.S. financial institutions, failed. The GDP and DJIA cratered, losing thirty and ninety percent, respectively. The election of Franklin Delano Roosevelt as President and his New Deal marked the turning point.

34 *See,* Appendix, "Changing New York."

however, and an outlier to the reform victories of new Mayor Fiorello LaGuardia, Dodge quickly fell back on the comfortable pursuits of minorities and the poor.

For weeks, D.A. Dodge's grand jury voted out petty crime indictments. But on May 13, 1935, Peckham's first prediction came true. Public opinion burst, and *men with determination and morality put the wrongdoers out.*

Manhattan's grand jury, led by foreman Lee Thompson Smith, barred Dodge and a junior assistant from their hearing room. They had heard enough street lottery ("numbers"), prostitution and bail bonding cases and demanded that the chief judge appoint a special prosecutor to investigate the highest levels of vice, racketeering and corruption.

There was a problem, though. Despite a list of names, no one wanted the job. Not one but two former federal prosecutors declined the offer. So did a former president of the New York City Bar Association. The son of a U.S. Supreme Court Justice also passed.

On June 2, 1935, Smith and the "runaway" grand jury, as D.A. Dodge was calling it, made another unprecedented move. They voted to disband.

Failing to see immediate responses from either Mayor LaGuardia or Police Commissioner Valentine, Foreman Smith offered parting words that must have stirred Peckham's ghost:

"It has become evident to us that the uncovering of organized crime is not a mere police routine but a major undertaking requiring a prosecutor of unusual vigor and ability to devote his entire energies and skill to combatting the apparently well organized and richly financed criminal forces."

By July 1, 1935, the call for Dewey, New York's former federal prosecutor had reached Albany, and Governor Herbert Lehman was (finally) for it. D.A. Dodge was not. Neither was Tammany Hall boss Jimmy Hines, not coincidentally. Despite their opposition, Lehman offered Dewey the job, and he accepted. In the words of one Dewey advisor, it was the "opportunity of a lifetime." In the words of the mafia, they thought Dewey "hopelessly mismatched."

Between July and October, Thomas Dewey, as if from Peckham's playbook, executed a level of *organization and coordination of forces* that harnessed a potent brand of public opinion, "civic outrage." He was likely unaware that it would also become his greatest protector.

Dewey began by severing all outside connections to avoid even the appearance of conflict. He transformed ten thousand square feet of space in the Woolworth Building, independent of Dodge's own offices. He employed phone operators, stenographers and law clerks outside of civil service pools and hired nearly a dozen accountants and more than seventy investigators.[35]

---

35 His most experienced man came from the staff of U.S. Treasury Secretary Henry Morgenthau, Jr., part of a growing contingent of influential supporters.

Getting to D.A.N.Y.

Dewey's legal team of twenty lawyers was a mix of those "young enough to have the vigor…[and] old enough to have the experience." All were highly educated. Frank S. Hogan, his later successor, was one of them. Commitments, in a nod to future arrangements, would last a year or two at most.

Dewey worked the intangibles, as well. He shrouded his efforts in secrecy and used it to create an indomitable aura. An agreeable press corps assisted. Through it all, Dewey's goal was clear: making "himself more frightening than the racketeers."

On July 30, 1935, he took to the radio for his first of many broadcasts, educating the public and fanning their desire for change. He also issued a broadside against his adversaries.

> *"The enemy was organized gangs of low-grade outlaws who lacked either the courage or the intelligence to earn an honest living. They succeed only so long as they can prey upon the fears and weaknesses of disorganized or timid witnesses. They fail, and run to cover, when business and the public, awakened to their own strength, stand up and fight."*

Dewey asked for the public's help and got it. Witnesses overloaded phone lines and deluged his office day and night. For the hundreds of leads, he empaneled one and then, by September 1935, another "extraordinary" grand jury. As he did, he aimed high and began taking out leaders of extortion and corrupt heads in labor and government.

He was, in all aspects, an efficient man for a sloppy city,[36] and while not officially, by that October, Manhattan's top prosecutor had changed addresses.

Wheeler Peckham would have been proud.

◆ ◆ ◆

Dewey's intended assassination was formulaic as far as mob hits went. Word was out that Dutch Schultz was a top Dewey target that fall. The two also had a history, Schultz enjoying the advantage with an upstate acquittal from Dewey's federal prosecutor days. When asked of Dewey's new position, Schultz crowed, "If the feds couldn't get me, I guess this fellow Dewey can't do much."

Schultz's confidence was short lived. Dewey, in perception and reality, was everywhere by then.

"I hope your ears fall off!" Schultz soon began shouting into the telephone, convinced (and rightly so) that his phones were tapped.

---

36 Everything about Dewey tailor made him for district attorney at that time. His successes would catapult him to the governor's office and later, twice, the Republican candidate for president. Ironically, the characteristics that made him such a success as a prosecutor and governor would undercut his presidential aspirations. His D.A. successor, Frank Hogan, would disagree. "The best man didn't win," Hogan would tell his staff the day after Dewey didn't defeat Truman in 1948. "Anyone who disagrees, I will personally throw through that window."

The October hit, Schultz explained to Charles "Lucky" Luciano and the mafia's governing Commission, would take advantage of Dewey's morning routine, killing him in the phone booth of his local pharmacy as he called into work.

Few liked the idea and unanimously voted Schultz down. Louis "Lepke" Buchalter, the Commission's co-chair thought it crazy and said as much.

"Bumping Dewey would be like setting fire to everything we have."

Schultz, enraged, accused them of stealing his territory and "feeding [him] to the law."

"Dewey's gotta go!" he yelled. "He's my nemesis. He's gotta go! I'm hitting him myself and in forty-eight hours!"

Schultz then stormed out.

That was October 23, 1935.

Whatever his intention, Schultz, in error, refocused the Commission's attention. They knew he'd begun to take out his own men out of fear of betrayal. After a six hour debate, they decided. By a vote of five to one, Schultz...not Dewey, would die.

At 10:00pm that night, Schultz, two body guards and his accountant were ambushed in the Palace Chop House in Newark, New Jersey. Schultz lived another twenty-two hours and then died at 8:00pm on October 24th. During that time, his remaining lieutenants were shot and killed in a Times Square barbershop and the Brooklyn Navy Yard.

The next morning, October 25, 1935, Dewey awoke to a new landscape.

The mafia had blinked.

Dewey's early accomplishments, like Peckham's speech, had their own foretelling. As Manhattan's chief prosecutor, Thomas Dewey would succeed thoroughly, and both he and the press soon forgot their earlier gag order. In doing so, the city and nation came to call him many things:

"The egomaniac."

"Sir Galahad of Owosso." (Michigan, his hometown.)

"Hitler in Boy Scout clothes." (*LIFE* magazine)

"That son of a bitch." (FDR)

"The little man on the wedding cake." (Alice Roosevelt Longworth)

But none stuck more than the one that emanated from the five foot, eight inch, mustachioed son of a newspaper man and grandson of an orator:

"The Gangbuster."

The legend that started with Dewey inspired a radio show in 1939, *Mr. District Attorney*. It aired the year after he officially became Manhattan's District Attorney and ran until 1952.

The program began with the "Voice of the Law," the show's opening feature and moral compass:

Voice of the Law:	*Mister District Attorney!*
	Champion of the people!
	Defender of the truth!
	Guardian of our fundamental rights to life, liberty and the pursuit of happiness!
Orchestra:	*[Theme, up full]*
[Echo Chamber]:	*…and it shall be my duty as district attorney not only to prosecute to the limit of the law all persons accused of crimes perpetrated within this county but to defend with equal vigor the rights and privileges of all its citizens.*

Forty years later, the voice reappeared for a television show, *Law & Order*:

> *"In the criminal justice system, the people are represented by two yet equally important groups: the police who investigate crime, and the district attorneys, who prosecute the offenders. These are their stories."*[37]

This time, though, it wasn't Dewey or Frank Hogan, D.A.N.Y.'s first patron saint. Serving as role model was the former lieutenant commander and federal prosecutor, Robert M. Morgenthau. Fifteen hundred lawyers wanted nothing more than to join his office each year.

In December 2000, I was one of them.

---

37 As the voice of *Law & Order*, Steven Zirnkilton holds the distinction of being the only actor to be in every episode of the flagship show and its three spin offs. In another bit of pop culture trivia, while it's his voice that became known for opening the show, it was missing from the pilot episode. Zirnkilton still got credit though as an onscreen detective!

Epilogue

The Manhattan D.A.'s Office

On the morning of my final interview with Mr. Morgenthau, my dad and I drove along Washington, D.C.'s beltway toward the Amtrak station. I'd resorted to the same suit and tie combo I'd worn to meet Ernie, the panel and Michelle Dylan. Hoping to please every bit of juju that remained, I wasn't altering a thing that day.

"Are you going to bring up Tumulty?" my dad asked.

The juju stirred.

"I'm not sure," I said.

Down juju. Down.

Joseph P. Tumulty was my great grandfather, my dad's grandfather and namesake. He was Governor and then President Woodrow Wilson's private secretary, a precursor position to chief of staff.

"You know he worked with Morgenthau's grandfather," my dad offered.

I knew.

Henry Morgenthau, Sr. had been ambassador to the Ottoman Empire under Wilson. Over the months of my speaking with friends and family about the Manhattan A.D.A. job, Tumulty found himself lashed to my pursuit whenever in earshot of my father.

"I bet he knows him."

I wasn't so sure. By the time Henry, Jr., Robert's father, worked for President Roosevelt, Tumulty had moved to the private sector, taking up a law practice in D.C. Considering the apocryphal story of the job candidate who had misplayed her final interview, images of my getting a blank stare or worse, resurrecting an unknown Morgenthau / Tumulty fallout, was very unappetizing.

But as my train moved through Maryland, then Delaware and toward New York and in between glances at my well-worn résumé and case law cheat sheet, the idea of talking family history with the legendary New Yorker began to look like a very cool opportunity.

Five hours later, when Mr. Morgenthau appeared, I rose to meet the man in the pictures I'd been staring at…but forty years older. The quick succession of his grip, his about-face and deep voice – "Come on back so we can talk a bit" – snapped me to. I would have crushed Robert M. Morgenthau in a foot race, but he was flat out faster.

His office was longer than it was wide and dated by wood paneling. Papers covered his desk in piles and under windows where blinds hung at different lengths. On the opposite wall, more pictures spanned the length of the room toward a conference table that ended by two standing flags, American and New York.

We made our way to the far end of the table. As we did, I thought of the four years, two countries, innumerable phone calls, letters and meetings and hours of travel and worry – legitimate *and* self-inflicted. I thought of my family, my friends and my mentors. I thought of my wife. I was likely getting a job. In New York City, too, where my only connections had been, until recently, the "I Love New York" jingle in between episodes of *The Love Boat* and *Magnum P.I.* twenty years earlier and University Pizza (The Bronx), Korean delis (Manhattan) and insane cabbies and bars in between while visiting friends in college.

Over the past eighteen months, it was looking up (way up) for The World Trade Center after I exited the *blue line* on Chambers so I'd know which way was south so I could head east to Centre and Hogan.

[I'd later discover better routes and, more embarrassingly, that New York trains didn't go by colors.]

Our conversation was brief. He asked me about law school and a few experiences. He then said without fanfare, "So, I'm offering you a spot."

I said I'd take it, and his delivery became rote.

"You'll receive some papers over the next few weeks. The only thing you have to do is pass the bar. We'll then see you in September."

I thanked him and said, "Of course." Rather than shake his hand and head for a pay phone, I paused.

"You know, my dad would kill me if I didn't ask you something," I began.

He didn't react.

I continued.

"Your father is Henry? Worked with President Roosevelt?"

Whether he was going to respond, it wasn't clear. I wasn't waiting.

"I think a relative of mine worked with him. Joseph Tumulty?"

His reaction was immediate. Slight surprise but with warmth.

"Oh sure, Joe Tumulty. He was very active in the party," Morgenthau said. "He was from New Jersey."

"He was," I said, although Morgenthau hadn't been asking.

He pushed away from the table.

"Let me show you something."

We moved toward one of the framed pictures on the wall, a black and white picture of President Roosevelt and Morgenthau's father. There, he paid a nice compliment to Tumulty. I don't remember exactly what.

I do remember that Robert Morgenthau, the Boss, now my boss, then extended his hand.

"I'll see you in a few months," he said.

Acknowledgements

C hapter Nine of the official *9/11 Commission Report* is titled, "Heroism and Horror." The opening paragraph reads, in part:

> *"On the morning of September 11, 2001, the last best hope for the community of people working in or visiting the World Trade Center rested not with the national policymakers but ... the first responders: fire, police, emergency medical service[.]"*

New York City Police Officer Kevin Lee did not die on 9/11. But that's the time when I came to know him, and I know he gave something that day alongside the four hundred and fourteen first responders who gave everything. I offer this personal story in his and their honor. Never forget.

Lucinda Franks, the Pulitzer Prize winning journalist and Robert Morgenthau's wife, used the following quote from a

Morgenthau colleague in her 2014 memoir, *Timeless: Love, Morgenthau and Me*:

> *"[Morgenthau] did the complete opposite of what was expected. Instead of hiring the white-shoe boys from Yale and Harvard, he'd take hungry imaginative students of minor law schools like St. John's in Queens, train them relentlessly, and set them free."*

She was quoting Victor Temkin about his getting hired when Morgenthau first became U.S. Attorney for the Southern District of New York. I'm a product of that thinking and am thankful for it.

My wife, Alyssa, has not just been supportive but my much needed reality check throughout our years of dating, marriage and friendship and my years working on (and returning to) this project. I love being married to her, and I'm still as thunder stuck today as I was back then.

The internet was incredibly useful, particularly researching the psychology of winning and losing and D.A.N.Y.'s history, but there was no comparison to walking around New York City, visiting the Lower East Side Tenement Museum and standing in the Baldizzi apartment in the fall of 2012 to get a sense of the 1930s. Seeing the bank calendar hanging on the wall and opened to October 1935 gave me chills. It was one of many winks from the universe that encouraged to keep at it.

Getting to D.A.N.Y.

Sitting for hours in the New York Public Library's Stephen A. Schwartzman Building looking at the photographs of Berenice Abbott's *Changing New York* portfolio was a time machine back to her own walks more than eighty years ago. If you cannot view it there, you can access it here: http://digitalcollections.nypl.org/collections/changing-new-york#/?tab=about

While the section "Changing New York" did not make the main body of *Getting to D.A.N.Y.* (it is now in the Appendix), I very much wanted to include it. An editorial golden rule rang through my head, though, and deserves mention, especially for those self-publishing – *kill your darlings*.

I want to thank some very helpful friends and family members, namely Barbara Caulfield, Phil Caulfield, Peter Clancy, Rob Clark, Walker Lamond, Nick Lopes, Andrea Stern and Chris and Melanie Schmidt. Getting their feedback on *Getting to D.A.N.Y.* validated what worked and sent me back to the drawing board to fix what didn't. If you like any of this, it's in large part because of them.

The lawyers who influenced me during law school may not know it, but they did: Michael Koby, William Rowan, Joseph Quirk, John Nalls, Paul Lane, Perry Paylor, Robert Ray and Elliott Berke. Before the lawyers, there was Pat McTeague; a new world, indeed.

Appendix

Outtake: "Changing New York"

On a fall morning in 1935, Adolfo Baldizzi awoke in his apartment on Manhattan's Lower East Side. Outside, the city and nation lay battered by the Great Depression. His wife Rosaria lay next to him. Both were illegal immigrants. His daughter Josephine and son Johnny, asleep nearby, were not. They were young Americans.

Around them, images of the Virgin Mary and Jesus, rosaries and crucifixes, pictures of mothers and fathers, grandmothers and grandfathers. And, of course, the President of the United States, completing the holy trinity of the time, religion, family and FDR.

Sixteen families occupied the top floors of the tenement at 97 Orchard Street. The Baldizzis' portion consisted of three rooms barely exceeding three hundred square feet, a single "efficiency" in the decades to come.

The kitchen was, literally, the center of their existence. A small table stood on new-to-market linoleum complete with rug-like design. The coin operated water heater, bars of soap, Bon Ami, Linit ("The Perfect Laundry Starch") and steel wool drew images of their olive skin rubbed raw as much as shirt collars ramrod straight.

Above the squat oven hung the prior day's laundry, dry and stiff. Nearby, a calendar from the Public National Bank and Trust Company of New York – a gift – either thanking Adolfo for his business or, more likely, asking for it.

Aldolfo had no business to give. No one needed a cabinet maker, however skilled. But dressed and fed, he moved along the narrow, poorly lit hall. Burlap covered the walls, collecting grime and soot, and added to the gloominess. Descending the stairs, he ran his hand down the bannister, dark and soft from so many others.

Adolfo would return hours later, unwanted and un-hired. Money for rent would continue to come from Rosaria's garment job and their Home Relief (welfare) benefits. It wouldn't matter. By year end, the landlord would evict them and every other family, choosing to empty the building rather than improve deteriorating conditions.

Outside, six blocks away, Berenice Abbott was a newly employed photographer of FDR's Works Progress Administration and New Deal. She was thirty-seven and a student of American artist Man Ray having learned from him while in Paris. Abbott was alone that October morning doing a bit of name making for herself and a changing New York.

She paused on the corner of Mercer and Houston Streets, SOHO in later and trendier times. A half dozen shacks huddled in the dirt and the shadow of a warehouse. Stove pipes jutted through roofs like periscopes and betrayed any sense the shanties were temporary. Tarpaulin and contact paper covered the doors to shield against the elements. Framed portraits and canvas landscapes hung everywhere, exposed, as if the walls inside were occupied by more cherished pieces.

Farthest from Abbott, a man sat on a wooden chair, reading, in a buttoned topcoat and fedora. Closer, stood the communal outhouse where another man exited. That man leaned down to the cupped hands of a third and accepted a fresh match for his cigarette. Two empty metal drums stood between the men and Abbott, one holding a fire to warm by, the other to cook.

Abbott raised her camera, focused and shot.

A few blocks north in a local pharmacy, Manhattan's recently appointed special prosecutor, Thomas E. Dewey, should have been lying in a pool of blood, dead, his breakfast still warm on the counter. But across the Hudson River in a Newark, New Jersey morgue, another body lay cold, twelve hours dead and a victim of a violent gangland murder.

The dead man, Arthur Flegenheimer, was better known as the gangster Dutch Schultz. He would never extort, bootleg or kill again. Dewey finished his meal and headed to his new fortress in the Woolworth Building at 233 Broadway, unaware of his good fortune.

The Manhattan D.A.'s Office calls 1935 the year of its modern birth.

October 25th was the day.

◆ ◆ ◆

For Baldizzi, October 25, 1935, was just another day attempting to provide for his family. He represented something more, though, and Berenice Abbott was canvassing the city capturing it on celluloid. Attitudes and resolve were materializing into concrete and steel, power and commerce.[38] There was an indisputable connection to the changes in the city's law and order.

Since the turn of the century, millions of immigrants flooded the city. The population doubled from three-and-a-half to seven

38 Berenice Abbott's work was part of the Federal Arts Project, a program of FDR's New Deal. Her portfolio, titled "A Changing New York", can be viewed in the New York Public Library's Stephen A. Schwartzman Building.

million newly arrived Germans, Jews, Italians and Catholics. An age (Gilded), an era (Progressive) and the Roaring 20s had passed. The Great Depression, into its sixth year, mercifully had bottomed out, and while the Baldizzis may not have felt it, recovery was underway.[39]

Abbott witnessed hard pressed men like the ones at Houston and Mott scraping together everything they could to survive. She saw them at places like Rothman's pawn shop on Eighth where they would "Call on Uncle," as the sign read, and collect loose change.

She watched them patronize a growing string of blue collar restaurants like Blossom's on Broadway and choose from pork chops, pig knuckles, lamb stews, oxtail goulash, Yankee pot roast and a misspelled "currey" of lamb at just $.15 to $.30 a plate. She couldn't help but see the contrast in the dying, multi-floor relics like Mori's in Greenwich Village with its muddied columns and stained façade.

For those who didn't build shanties, Abbott saw them using hideouts like the Lyric Theatre on Third Avenue, paying $.10 for shelter. With sailors, drunks and actual moviegoers they watched

---

39 Between 1932 and 1933, unemployment hit twenty-five percent, which accounted for thirteen million people out of work. Average household incomes dropped forty percent, and the federal government counted more than sixty percent of all Americans as poor. Eleven thousand banks, almost forty-five percent of all U.S. financial institutions, failed. The GDP and DJIA cratered, losing thirty and ninety percent, respectively. The election of Franklin Delano Roosevelt and his New Deal marked the turning point.

movies like "The Law of the 45s (Where Blood Flowed Red!)" with Charlie Chaplin and Big Boy William, news reels and shorts.

More impressively, though, Abbott saw these people not so much finding but *creating* work. They took to push carts, some fourteen thousand, and peddled Chiclets, Baby Ruth, fruits and vegetables, baked sweet potatoes, roasted chestnuts and roasted corn, hot dogs and soft drinks. They stood in newsstands and sold Horton's Ice Cream, Bit-O-Honey and Nestles, *Science and Mechanics*, *Flying Aces*, *True Detective*, *Redbook*, *Colliers* and the *Saturday Evening Post*.

They built and then drove automobiles like the Buick Eight, Auburn Speedster and Graham Paige, crowding alongside and then ending the reigns of horse drawn wagons and trolleys. They built and then drove over the Brooklyn, Williamsburg, Manhattan and 59th Street bridges and then dug the Holland, erected the George Washington and began the Triborough. In doing so, they created new traffic systems and birthed for millions of poor bastards to come the daily New York commute.

They didn't stop there.

As Abbott walked along the island's surrounding waters, she photographed them as they manned tugboats like the *Watuppa* and cleared lanes of winter ice and summer congestion and steamers and freightliners moved eighteen million tons of wheat, coal, lumber and iron, and companies like Union Refrigerator Transit

Co. and Standard Fruit & Steamship Co. sought ports from Central America, the Caribbean and West Indies.

Winding through Lower and then Midtown Manhattan, she took photograph after photograph.

Civil War era homes and carriage houses gave way to the likes of the Waldorf-Astoria, Radio City Music Hall and Rockefeller Center. The Bank of Manhattan Trust, Chrysler and Empire State gave architecture a new term, "sky scraper". In them and throughout the city, the burgeoning workforce – in banking, trade, art, media and communication – propelled New York City, no longer London, to become the financial capital of the world.

But in the streets where unchecked crime and self-dealing had perverted government, law and order, they did something monumentally more important.

They laid the foundation for another change. In the words of D.A. Peckham from 1901, <u>they</u> were the power *that would overcome present conditions.*

Bibliography & Suggested Reading

Abbott, Berenice, As Photographed By. *New York In The Thirties.* Dover, 1973.

Caro, Robert A. *The Power Broker, Robert Moses and the Fall of New York.* Vintage Books, 1975.

Conlon, Edward. *Blue Blood.* Riverhead Books, 2004.

Franks, Lucinda. *Timeless; Love, Morgenthau and Me.* Sarah Crichton Books, 2014.

Morris, Edmund. *Theodore Rex.* The Modern Library, 2002.

Puzo, Mario. *The Godfather.* G.P. Putnam Sons, 1969.

Smith, Richard Norton. *Thomas E. Dewey and His Times.* Simon and Schuster, 1982.

Thomas, Evan. *The Man to See. Edward Bennett Williams, Ultimate Insider; Legendary Trial Lawyer.* Simon & Schuster, 1991.

Turow, Scott. *One L.* Farrar Straus Giroux, 1977.

Other Reference

Boldero, Jennifer M. and Francis, Jillian J. "Emotional Responses to Self-Evaluation: The Influence of Situation and Self-System Characteristics", *Psychology of Moods*. Nova Science, 2005.

Dunning, John. *On the Air: The Encyclopedia of Old Time Radio*. Oxford University, 1998.

Durst, John E., Jr. and Fuchsberg, Abraham. *New York Courtroom Evidence*. Lexis Publishing, 2000.

Medvec, Victoria Husted; Madey, Scott F.; Gilovich, Thomas. "When Less is More: Counterfactual Thinking and Satisfaction Among Olympic Medalists", *Journal of Personality and Social Psychology*, October 1995.

New York Criminal Statutes and Rules. LexisNexis, 2005.

About the Author

Paul Caulfield was born in Washington, D.C., in 1974. He graduated from Fairfield University in 1996 and worked as a Catholic missionary between 1996 and 1997 in Durán, Ecuador. After returning to Washington, D.C., he taught religion, grammar and creative writing at Annunciation Catholic School before entering The Catholic University of America's Columbus School of Law and graduating in 2001. From 2001 to 2004, he was an Assistant District Attorney in the New York County District Attorney's Office, where he investigated and prosecuted a variety of street and white collar crimes. Between 2006 and 2007, in a major pro bono effort, he wrote extensively and appeared nationally on cable news programs as one of the earliest legal analysts critical of then-North Carolina District Attorney Michael Nifong for his false prosecution that became nationally known as the "Duke lacrosse rape" case.

Today, he is the chief compliance officer at an international private and commercial bank. Caulfield lives with his wife, Alyssa, and three children in Northport, Long Island.

Made in the USA
Coppell, TX
27 January 2022

72460582R00085